TEXTS AND TRANSLATION

PSEUDEPIGRAPHA SERIES

3

THE HEBREW FRAGMENTS OF PSEUDO-PHILO'S

LIBER ANTIQUITATUM BIBLICARUM

PRESERVED IN THE *CHRONICLES OF JERAHMEEL*

Edited and translated by

Daniel J. Harrington

SOCIETY OF BIBLICAL LITERATURE

1974

THE HEBREW FRAGMENTS OF PSEUDO-PHILO'S

LIBER ANTIQUITATUM BIBLICARUM

PRESERVED IN THE *CHRONICLES OF JERAḤMEEL*

Copyright © 1974

by

The Society of Biblical Literature

Library of Congress Catalog Card Number: 73-89170

ISBN: 088414-036-9

Printed in The United States of America
Printing Department, University of Montana
Missoula, Montana 59801

PREFACE TO THE SERIES

TEXTS AND TRANSLATIONS is a project of the Committee on
Research and Publications of the Society of Biblical Literature
and is under the general direction of George W. MacRae (Harvard
Divinity School), Executive Secretary, and Harry M. Orlinsky
(Hebrew Union College-Jewish Institute of Religion, New York),
Chairman of the Committee. The purpose of the project is to make
available in convenient and inexpensive format ancient texts
which are not easily accessible but are of importance to scholars
and students of "biblical literature" as broadly defined by the
Society. Reliable modern English translations will accompany the
texts. Occasionally the various series will include documents
not published elsewhere. It is not a primary aim of these publications to provide authoritative new critical texts, nor to
furnish extensive annotations. The editions are regarded as
provisional, and individual volumes may be replaced in the future
as better textual evidence becomes available. The following
subseries have been established thus far:

   PSEUDEPIGRAPHA, edited by Robert A. Kraft (University of
        Pennsylvania)

   GRECO-ROMAN RELIGION, edited by Hans Dieter Betz (School of
        Theology at Claremont)

   EARLY CHRISTIAN LITERATURE, edited by Birger A. Pearson
        (University of California at Santa Barbara)

For the PSEUDEPIGRAPHA SERIES the choice of texts is governed
in part by the research interests of the SBL Pseudepigrapha Group,
of which George W. E. Nickelsburg, Jr. (University of Iowa) is
currently Chairman and James H. Charlesworth (Duke University)
Secretary. This series will focus on Jewish materials from the
Hellenistic era and will regularly include volumes that
incorporate the fragmentary evidence of works attributed to

biblical personalities, culled from a wide range of Jewish and
Christian sources. The volumes are selected, prepared, and
edited in consultation with the following editorial subcommittee
of the Pseudepigrapha Group:

Sebastian P. Brock (Cambridge University, England)

George W. MacRae (Harvard Divinity School)

George W. E. Nickelsburg, Jr. (University of Iowa)

Michael E. Stone (Hebrew University, Israel)

John Strugnell (Harvard Divinity School)

Robert A. Kraft, Editor

TABLE OF CONTENTS

ACKNOWLEDGEMENTS

The editor-translator wishes to express his
gratitude to the Curators of the Bodleian
Library for permission to publish selections
from MS. Heb. d. 11, to John Strugnell and
Robert A. Kraft for editorial suggestions,
and to Carol Cross for typing the manuscript.

INTRODUCTION

The *Chronicles of Jerahmeel* (hereafter *CJ*), a 14th century manuscript (MS. Heb. d. 11) preserved in the Bodleian Library, was com-
piled by Rabbi Eleazar ben Asher the Levite in the Rhine provinces.
Almost all of the text was translated into English by Moses Gaster
in 1899.[1] *CJ* contains among other things extracts and paraphrases
in Hebrew corresponding to the Latin text of Pseudo-Philo's *Liber
Antiquitatum Biblicarum* (hereafter *LAB*), a history of Israel from
Adam to David.[2] *LAB* was composed in Hebrew, probably before A.D.
100,[3] translated into Greek and then into Latin; only the Latin version survives.

This volume presents the Hebrew texts of *CJ* which correspond to
Pseudo-Philo's *Liber Antiquitatum Biblicarum* along with a new English
translation of these Hebrew fragments. The texts from *CJ* are cited
according to the numeration found in Gaster's translation while the
references to *LAB* correspond to the numeration established by M. R.
James and followed in the main by Guido Kisch. The volume should be
useful as a tool for discussing the textual history of *LAB*, for
tracing the influence of *LAB*, and for investigating the background
of *CJ*.

The first twenty-five chapters of *CJ* deal with creation, the
formation of the child, hell, paradise, and the early history of man-
kind. We join *LAB* in *CJ* 26-30 (MS. Heb. d. 11 22r-25v) which corre-
sponds to *LAB* 1-7. We have the genealogy from Adam to Noah; the
genealogy from Cain to Lamech; God's speech in response to Noah's
sacrifices; the list of the sons of Japhet, Ham and Shem along with
a list of Abraham's ancestors; the review of Noah's descendants; the

---

[1]Moses Gaster, *The Chronicles of Jerahmeel Or, The Hebrew Bible
Historiale*, Oriental Translation Fund, New Series IV (London, 1899);
revised edition with a 124 pp. prolegomenon by Haim Schwarzbaum (New
York: Ktav, 1971). Emphasizing the folklore background of *CJ*,
Schwarzbaum's introduction is a substantial work in itself. His
bibliography on pp. 112-124 is especially valuable.

[2]Guido Kisch, *Pseudo-Philo's Liber Antiquitatum Biblicarum*, Publications in Mediaeval Studies 10 (Notre Dame, 1949). For an English translation, see M. R. James, *The Biblical Antiquities of Philo*,
Translations of Early Documents Series I, Palestinian Jewish Texts
(London, 1917); revised edition with a 169 pp. prolegomenon by Louis
H. Feldman (New York: Ktav, 1971). See especially Feldman's bibliography, pp. CLVI-CLXI. A new edition of the Latin text with French
translation and commentary will be published for the Philo collection
of *Sources chrétiennes* by D. J. Harrington, P.-M. Bogaert and C.
Perrot.

[3]See my articles, "The Original Language of Pseudo-Philo's
Liber Antiquitatum Biblicarum," *Harvard Theological Review* 63 (1970)
503-514; "The Biblical Text of Pseudo-Philo's *Liber Antiquitatum
Biblicarum*," *Catholic Biblical Quarterly* 33 (1971) 1-17.

tower of Babel and Abraham's rescue from the fire; and the confusion
brought about in building the tower. We rejoin *LAB* 9 again in *CJ*
42.5-9 (MS. Heb. d. 11 37v) which recounts Amram's refusal to despair
during the afflictions in Egypt, Miriam's dream, and the birth of
Moses. Finally, in *CJ* 57-59 (MS. Heb. d. 11 58r-61v) we have selections which are concerned with the exploits of Kenaz (*LAB* 25-28),
the deeds of Ja'el (*LAB* 31.3-8), Gideon's demand for a sign (*LAB*
35.6-7), the deeds of Jair (*LAB* 38.1-4), the victories of Jephthah
and the sacrifice of his daughter (*LAB* 39-40), the deception of Micah
(*LAB* 44), and the war between Israel and Benjamin along with the de-
parture of Phineas (*LAB* 46-48). *CJ* 60-100 continues the history of
Israel down to the death of Judah the Maccabee.

The Relation Between CJ *and* LAB

In the introduction to his English translation of *CJ*, Moses
Gaster contended that in *CJ* we have the original Hebrew text of *LAB*.[4]
Decisive for Gaster were the forms of proper names. If the original
Hebrew of *LAB* were translated into Greek and then into Latin and then
back into Hebrew (= *CJ*), he reasoned that the differences between ה
and ח, ט and ת, כ and ק, א and ע as well as among שׂ, ס and צ would
have disappeared. If the Hebrew text were a translation from Latin,
none of these double letters or letters representing peculiar Semitic
sounds which were not distinctly noted in Latin or Greek could be
expected to reappear correctly in the Hebrew text. Yet in the list
of names given in *CJ* 26.2 (= *LAB* 1.3): עֲלִי שָׁאֵל צוּרִי עלמיאל בָּרוּךְ כעל
נחת וזרחמה צשא מחתל וענת ('Elî, Še'el, Ṣûrî, 'Elmî'el, Berôk, Ke'al,
Naḥat, Zarḥamah, Ṣiša, Maḥtal and 'Anat) the distinctions between
the letters are carefully observed. According to Gaster, anyone
retroverting from a Latin text could not have been so skilled and so
accurate that he would have kept these distinctions. Gaster also
found what he considered to be mistranslations of *CJ* in *LAB*. He
argued that in *CJ* 27.4 ובני is a proper name *Wābnî* mistakenly read
as *ûbenê* and rendered as *et filii* ("and the sons") in *LAB* 4.6. In
CJ 28.3 instead of 640, *LAB* 5.3 has 340; the translator into Greek
or Latin must have read שלש for שש. Finally in *CJ* 29.13 where the
Hebrew text has "appeased the wrath of the people," *LAB* 6.16 has
liquefactus; the translator read וישפך for וישכך of *CJ*. Therefore,
Gaster concludes that the Hebrew text in *CJ* cannot be a translation
from a non-Semitic original and that the Latin *LAB* can only be

---

[4]Gaster, pp. xxx-xxxix.

considered as a faithful but secondary translation.[5]

Leopold Cohn, in response to Gaster, maintained that the Hebrew sections of *CJ* corresponding to *LAB* are not the original text but rather are fragments retroverted from a Latin manuscript.[6] Gaster's argument that accuracy in maintaining distinctions between Hebrew letters which merge in the Greek and Latin alphabets rules out the possibility of retroversion from Latin to Hebrew, is simply unsound. To a man learned in the Bible and skilled in Hebrew language, accurate retroversion from Latin to Hebrew of proper names would present little real difficulty. Such a man could even be expected to supply learned corrections. Furthermore, how does Gaster know which names are correct and which are not? The passage cited is not a biblical quotation, and the names are often unknown and implausible. Also, many names found in *CJ* are best understood as the result of translation. According to Cohn, it is impossible that the Hebrew original of *LAB* could have had such un-Hebraic forms as do appear in *CJ*. Moreover, Cohn feels that there are examples of textual corruption in the manuscript history of *LAB* which are reproduced in *CJ*. Cohn, then, has argued that the *LAB* sections contained in *CJ* are retroversions from the Latin and do not represent the original Hebrew version. Haim Schwarzbaum has agreed with Cohn that the compiler of *CJ* has inserted into his anthology Hebrew fragments and abridgements from the Latin *LAB*. He states: "I cannot endorse Gaster's theory that the Pseudo-Philo items incorporated in Jeraḥmeel constitute the original text (or *Urtext*) of the *Liber Antiquitatum Biblicarum*."[7]

It is possible that the limits of the debate (Hebrew original or retroversions from the Latin) have been too narrow. After all, the *CJ* fragments could be a translation from Greek or could represent a different Hebrew recension (the example of the Hebrew texts of Sirach comes to mind). Yet there does seem to be decisive evidence that the fragments preserved in *CJ* do not represent the original Hebrew of *LAB*. This evidence is the presence of certain readings in *CJ* which reflect errors most readily explainable at the level of Latin. (1) *CJ* 27.3 (= *LAB* 4.3-4) has אז נפצה שליש ארץ רומירת: ויכבשו בניו את ידיד (Then a third of the land of Rômêret was separated off. And his sons conquered Yadêd). *LAB* has *tunc divisa est pars tercia terre. Domereth et filii eius acceperunt Ladech*

---

[5]Gaster, p. xxxvi.

[6]Leopold Cohn, "Pseudo-Philo und Jerachmeel," *Festschrift zum siebzigsten Geburtstage Jakob Guttmans* (Leipzig, 1915), pp. 173-185.

[7]Schwarzbaum, p. 6.

(And then the third part of the earth was divided. Gomer and his sons took Ladech). The key word here is רומירת/*Domereth*. According to Gen 10.2-4 we should expect the name *Gomer*. The *-eth* ending is the Latin *et* which has become fused with the Latin name *Gomer* (= *Domer*), and then another *et* was necessarily added. The Hebrew retroverter did not recognize that a mistake had occurred in the Latin, and so he merely reproduced it. Furthermore, he misread the sentence and so concluded the sentence after *Domereth*. (2) *CJ* 28.3 (= *LAB* 5.4) has תחת ידו while *LAB* has *secundum sceptra ducationum suarum* (or the like). It is incredible that the complex Latin phrase could have developed out of תחת ידו while, on the other hand, it is reasonable to suppose that תחת ידו does represent an attempt to retrovert the obscure Latin of *LAB*. *LAB* may be based on a Hebrew original close to that of Lev 27.32 כל אשר יעבר תחת השבט. (3) *CJ* 30.3 (= *LAB* 7.3) has אקרבם בצינות, while *LAB* has *in scuto approximabo eos* ("I will liken them to a shield"). In *LAB* the phrase appears in parallelism with *tamquam stillicidium arbitrabor eos* ("I will consider them like a drop of water"). The expressions are undoubtedly citations of Isa 40.15c, and so James's emendation (pp. 95, 247) of *scuto* ("shield") to *sputo* ("spittle") must be correct. The expression is based on Isa 40.15c where *LAB* reads with LXX σίελος (= ריר) against the MT's דק; the emendation is confirmed by *4 Ezra* 6.56, *2 Baruch* 82.5 and *LAB* 12.4 *(Et erit mihi hominum genus tamquam stillicidium urcei, et tamquam sputum estimabitur)*. *CJ*'s בצינות suggests that a mistake possible only in Latin (*scuto* for *sputo*) had already occurred before *LAB* was retroverted into Hebrew. The verb אקרבם seems to be an attempt to make sense out of the corruption; we would expect the root דמה.

Comparison of the Hebrew in *CJ* with some passages from the Hebrew Bible confirms our view that we are dealing with retroversions. (1) *CJ* 26.9 (= *LAB* 1.20) has ינחמנו ריניח ("This one will comfort us and give rest") while *LAB* has *hic requiem dabit nobis* ("This one will give rest to us"). The retroverter has harmonized the biblical text of *LAB* with that of the MT. While *LAB* 1.20 with its *hic requiem dabit nobis* preserves the LXX reading, *CJ* 26.9 (ינחמנו ריניח) combines the LXX and MT readings. Since there is no *LAB* manuscript evidence whatever for ינחמנו, it can be explained as just the kind of reading which a retroverter, familiar with the MT, and embarrassed by the LXX reading, would add. (2) *CJ* 27.5 (= *LAB* 4.10) has את שלפטרא ואת מוזאם וריאדורא ועוזים דיקלבל מימואל שַבִיטְחָפִין, *LAB* has *Salastra et Muzaam, Rea, Dura, Uzia, Deglabal, Mimoel, Sabthfin.* Both these texts are lists of names taken originally from

Gen 10.26-9. When these lists are compared with the biblical lists of Yoqtan's sons (Sheleph, Hazarmaveth, Jerah, Hadoram, Uzal, Diklah, Obal, Abimael, Sheba, Ophir), both appear to be quite corrupt. The list in *CJ* is so corrupt that we could hardly imagine a Hebrew author doing such a bad job of reproducing the Hebrew Bible. On the other hand, the situation is perfectly understandable if we suppose that a translator failed to recognize the corrupt Latin list actually is Gen 10.26-9 or felt bound to translate mechanically what he found before him.

When the examples cited here are coupled with the weakness of Gaster's counterargument described above, then we can only conclude that the fragments in *CJ* represent a translation of the Latin *LAB*.

CJ, however, is difficult to use as a textual witness for *LAB*. Much of it (especially in chaps. 57-59) seems to be paraphrase rather than translation. It is often impossible to determine the Latin reading through the medium of Hebrew. There is, as we have seen, some tendency toward standardizing to the MT. Moreover, most of the good conjunctive errors in *LAB* occur in the sections omitted in *CJ*. In short, we cannot say with absolute certainty what type of *LAB* MS the translator had at his disposal. In fact, he could have used more than one MS and sifted out many of the distinctive conjunctive errors.

This is not the place to set out the whole stemma of the Latin MSS of *LAB*, but we can at least sketch it briefly to set the stage for our discussion of *CJ* as a textual witness.[8] The eighteen complete and three fragmentary MSS of *LAB* are to be divided into two major groups: (Δ) = Fulda-Cassel Theol. 4°, 3, Phillips 461, Phillips 391, Trèves 117; (Π) = (sub-group β) Budapest Cod. lat. 23, Vatican Lat. 448, Würzburg 276, Munich 18481, Munich 17133, Munich 4569, Fitzwilliam McClean 31; (sub-group δ) Admont 359, Salzburg a. VII 17, Rein 55; (sub-group θ) Berlin Görres 132, Cues 16, Göttweig 246 (254b), Melk 324, Trèves 71/1055, Vienna Lat. 446. Δ is higher on the stemma than Π.

Can we determine the textual value of *CJ* as a witness to *LAB*? Does it belong to Π or Δ? Unfortunately, we cannot argue from conjunctive errors here; we must resort to distinctive readings. These

---

[8]For a full discussion of the significance of *CJ* for the MSS tradition of *LAB*, see the introduction to the forthcoming edition to be published in the Philo collection of *Sources chrétiennes*. For a preliminary report on the *LAB* MSS see my article "The Text-Critical Situation of Pseudo-Philo's *Liber Antiquitatum Biblicarum*," *Revue Bénédictine* 83 (1973) 383-388.

6

are the most important agreements between *CJ* and *LAB*.

(1) *LAB* 1.4 Sifatecia Δ Sifa Tetia Π; *CJ* 26.2 זִיפַח הִיכִיאָה‎ = Π

(2) *LAB* 1.6 Malida Δ Malila Π; *CJ* 26.3 מְלִילָא‎ = Π

(3) *LAB* 2.8 uxores Δ uxorem Π; *CJ* 26.15 אשת‎ = Π

(4) *LAB* 4.6 Filii Ethii Chus Δ Et hi filii Chus Π; *CJ* 27.4 ואלה בני כוש‎ = Π

(5) *LAB* 4.6 Et filii Sidona Δ Et filii Canaan Sidona Π; *CJ* 27.4 ורבני כנען צידון‎ = Π

(6) *LAB* 4.8 Segom Δ Seboim Π; *CJ* 27.4 צבוים‎ = Π

(7) *LAB* 4.12 Abielobth Δ Abiel Obthi Π; *CJ* 27.6 אביאל עובד‎ = Π

(8) *LAB* 4.14 Recap Dediap Berechap Δ Recab Dediab Berechab Π; *CJ* 27.7 רכב דדיאב בריכב‎ = Π

(9) *LAB* 5.5 (Et filii Canaan)... XXXII milia DCCC Δ XXXII milia DCCCC Π; *CJ* 28.4 ורבני כנען שנים ושלשים אלף ותשע מאות‎ = Π

(10) *LAB* 6.7 et sustinete eos ibidem Δ et sustinete cum eis ibidem Π; *CJ* 29.7 ותחיו עמהם שם‎ = Π

(11) *LAB* 6.8 (Et adduxerunt viros) a domo eius Δ ad domum eius Π; *CJ* 29.8 ויביאום לפני יקטן‎ = Π

(12) *LAB* 7.2 lingua una Δ lingua una omnibus Π; *CJ* 30.2 שפה אחת לכולם‎ = Π

(13) *LAB* 9.8 et lumen sempiternum luceam ei Δ et lumen sempiternum luceat et Π; *CJ* 42.7 ואור עולם תאיר לו‎ = Π

(14) *LAB* 9.9 uxorem de tribu sua Δ mulierem stirpis sue nomine Jacobe Π; *CJ* 42.8 ויקח את יוכבד בת לוי אשתו‎ = Π

(15) *LAB* 25.9 monte Abrahe...absconsa sunt sub Π; omit Δ by haplography; *CJ* 57.11-12 = Π

(16) *LAB* 25.11 He sunt sancte nimphe Δ Et he sunt nimphe Π; *CJ* 57.13 והמה העצבים‎ = Π

(17) *LAB* 26.3 postquam concremaverit ignis homines istos Δ postquam concremaveris homines istos Π; *CJ* 57.18 כאשר תשרמם‎ = Π

(18) *LAB* 26.15 et sunt usque in hodiernum diem Δ et sunt ibi usque in hodiernum diem Π; *CJ* 57.25 ויהיו שם עד הירם הזה‎ = Π

(19) *LAB* 27.9 videntes dixerunt Δ videntes Amorrei dixerunt Π; *CJ* 57.33 ויראו האמורי ויאמרו‎ = Π

(20) *LAB* 27.9 hec est romphea Cenez Δ ecce romphea Cenez Π; *CJ* 57.33 הנה חרב קנז‎ = Π

(21) *LAB* 27.15 Quid nos interrogas? Quod nos interrogas? Δ Quid nos interrogas Π; *CJ* 57.37 למה זה תשאל לנו‎ = Π

(22) *LAB* 28.5 parcat...sue Δ parcet...sue hereditati sue Π; *CJ* 57.38 יחמול יי על נחלתו‎ = Π

(23) *LAB* 40.6 corona Δ flores corone Π; *CJ* 59.7 פרחי כתרי‎ = Π

(24) *LAB* 40.4 et abiens decidet in sinum matrum suarum Π; omit Δ;
      CJ 59.6 וחבא שְׁאֵילָה בת יפחח וחשטח בחיק אמה = Π

(25) *LAB* 40.8 filii Israel Δ filie Israel Π; *CJ* 59.8 בנות ישראל = Π

(26) *LAB* 44.5 effigies tres puerorum et vitulorum Δ effigies tres
      puerorum et tres vitulorum Π; *CJ* 59.12 שלש צלמי אדם ושלשה צלמי
      עגלים = Π

These examples would seem to suggest that *CJ* should definitely be
placed with the Π group. But there are other examples where *CJ*
agrees with Δ; some of these (*LAB* 5.5 = *CJ* 28.4; *LAB* 6.14 = *CJ* 29.12;
LAB 28.8 = *CJ* 57.41) are significant.

(1) *LAB* 1.14 Anac Δ Anas Π; *CJ* 26.7 ענק = Δ

(2) *LAB* 4.14 Ceneta Δ Cene Etha Π; *CJ* 27.7 קניטא = Δ

(3) *LAB* 4.16 Seruch autem et filii eius Δ Seruch autem et filie
     eius Π (filii BCDO); *CJ* 27.9 ושרוג ובניר = Δ

(4) *LAB* 5.5 (Filii vero Sabaca)...XLVI milia CCCC Δ XXXVI milia
     CCCC Π; *CJ* 28.4 בני סבחכא ששה וארבעים אלף וארבע מאות = Δ

(5) *LAB* 6.4 dixerunt Δ dixerunt ad illos Π; *CJ* 29.3 ויאמרו = Δ

(6) *LAB* 6.14 Frangentes fregerunt Δ Frangentes fregerunt vincula Π;
     CJ 29.12 שברו = Δ

(7) *LAB* 7.2 et dixit Δ et dixit Deus Π; *CJ* 30.2 ויאמר = Δ

(8) *LAB* 28.8 scintilla ascendit Δ scintilla descendit Π; *CJ* 57.41
     ניצוץ עלה = Δ

(9) *LAB* 28.8 annis septem milia Δ annis quatuor milia Π; *CJ* 57.41
     שבעת אלפי שנים = Δ

No conclusion can be drawn. The author of *CJ* could have used an
early MS, and so *CJ* could possibly witness a stage in transmission
prior to the division into two major groups. On the other hand,
the author could have used more than one MS.

This Edition

This edition presents the Hebrew texts from *CJ* along with new
English translations on facing pages. *CJ* is cited according to
Gaster's numeration, and *LAB* is referred to according to the James/
Kisch scheme. *CJ* references accompany the Hebrew, and *LAB* references accompany the English. Biblical quotations are italicized in
the translation. Proper names are transliterated according to
their form in the *Revised Standard Version* (RSV). Where a proper
name is not found in the Bible, we have spelled the name according
to its vocalization in the *CJ* text; where there is no vocalization,
we have been guided first by *LAB* and then by Gaster. Where there
is a significant difference between *CJ* and *LAB*, the reading of *LAB*
is cited in the notes; where *LAB* sheds light on a translation, its
text is also cited in the notes.

Critical signs employed in the text and translation:

⌐ ⌐	text of MS seems to be corrupt
[ ]	lacuna in MS
( )	words or letters supplied by editor, although there is no actual lacuna in the MS
. . . .	words seem to be missing, although there is no actual lacuna in the MS
{ }	suggested deletion of material that is present in the MS
< >	explanation or alternative rendering supplied by editor

The present translation is a new one which aims at a literal
rendering of the Hebrew text. The translator has consulted Gaster's
translation as well as the Latin text of *LAB*.

26.1   אדם הוליד שלשה בנים ושלש בנות קין ותאומתו קַלְמָנָא אשתו והבל
ותאומתו דבורה אשתו ושת ותאומתו נוֹבָא אשתו:

2   ויחי אדם אוחרי הולידו את שת שבע מאות ויולד בנים אחד עשר ובנות
שמנה:

=1.3   ואלה שמות בניו עֲלִי שָׁאַל צגְּרַי עלמיאל בָּרוֹך כעל נחת זרחמה צשא
מחתל וענת:

=1.4   ושם הבנות חוה גיטש חַרְיִיבִיבָّא זיפת הָיכִיאה שַׁבָּא עַזַין:

3   ויחי שת מאה וחמש שנה ויולד את אנוש: ויחי שת אחרי הולידו את
אנוש שבע מאות ושבע שנה ויולד בנים שלשה ושתי בנות:

=1.6   ושם הבנים אלִיְדַעַה פוּנָא ומַתַח ושם הבנות מָלִילַא וָתִילַא:

4   ויחי אנוש מאה ושמונים שנה ויולד את קינן: ויחי אנוש אחרי
הולידו את קינן .... שני בנים אָהור רָאַל ובת אחת קַטִינָת:

5   וקינן הוליד אחרי מהללאל ג׳ בנים התך מוכבו ולופא רב בנות חנה
לליבא:

6   ומחללאל הוליד אחרי ירד ז׳ בנים טֵיקָא מָאיַא צִיבַּר מִילִי אֲאַש אוריאל
לוראוטין רֹה בנות עדה נועה יָבַל מעדה צלה:

7   ירד הוליד אחרי חנוך ד׳ בנים לעיעד ענק סבכי יתר רב בנות זַזכֹ
עֲוַה:

8   חנוך הוליד אחרי מתושלח הֹ בנים עַנַז לִיאוֹן עַכַורַוֹן פְלֵידי אֲלִידי רֹג
בנות תַאיַיז לִיפֵיד לַאיַיַאד ויחפוץ יי בחנוך ויקחהו:

9   מת{ מתושלח (הוליד) אחרי למך בנים ב׳ ובנות ב׳ עינב רפוא עלומה
עָמוּבָה:

=1.20 ולמך הוליד את נח לאמר זה ינחמנו ויניח לארץ ולכל אשר עליה כי
יפקד יי רעה על הארץ למען החמס אשר ברעועים:

---

[1] *CJ* and *LAB* along with LXX have 700 years; MT, Samaritan and Jubilees have 800 years.

[2] MT has a slightly different form: חמש שנים ומאה שנה.

[3] MT has a different form: שבע שנים ושמנה מאות שנה. Again *CJ* and *LAB* agree with LXX (707) against MT, Sam and Jub (807).

[4] The LXX has 190 and the MT 90; *LAB* also has 180.

[5] *LAB* has *annos DCCXV et genuit* in this place.

[6] *LAB*'s *et Leva* suggests ולִיבא.

[7] In the *CJ* MS there is a false start -מת, then the proper name; but the verb has been omitted.

1.1   Adam fathered three sons and three daughters: Cain and his
         twin, Qalmanā', his wife; and Abel and his twin, Deborah,
         his wife; and Seth and his twin, Nōbā', his wife,

1.2   And *Adam* lived, *after he had fathered Seth, 700 (years)*[1]
         and he fathered eleven *sons and* eight *daughters*   (Gen 5.4).

1.3   And these are the names of his sons: 'Elî, Še'el, Ṣûrî,
         'Elmî'el, B^{e}rôk, Ke'al, Naḥat, Zarḥamah, Siša', Maḥtal and
         'Anat.

1.4   And the name(s) of the daughters: Ḥawāh, Gîṭaš, Harêbîka',
         Zîpat, Hêki'ah, Šaba', 'Azîn.

1.5   *And Seth lived* 105 years[2] *and fathered Enosh; and Seth lived*
         after he had fathered Enosh, 707 years[3] *and he fathered*
         three *sons and two daughters*   (Gen 5.6-7).

1.6   And the name(s) of the sons: 'Elîde'ah, Pûna' and Matat;
         and the name(s) of the daughters: M^{e}lîla' and Tîla'.

1.7-8   *And Enosh lived* 180 years[4] *and he fathered Kenan; and Enosh*
         lived, after he had fathered Kenan (Gen 5.9-10)....[5] two
         sons: 'Ehôr and 'A'al; and one daughter: Qaṭênat.

1.9-10   And Kenan fathered after Mahalalel (see Gen 5.12-13) three
         sons: Hatak, Mōkkō and Lûpa'; and two daughters: Ḥannah,
         L^{e}liba.[6]

1.11-12 And Mahalalel fathered, after Yared (see Gen 5.15-16),
         seven sons: Ṭêqa', Mā'ya', Ṣêkar, Mêlî, 'A'eš, 'Ûrî'el,
         Lûr'ûṭîn; and five daughters: 'Adah, Nô'ah, Yebal, Ma'adah,
         Ṣillah.

1.13-14 Yared fathered, after Enoch (see Gen 5.18-19), four sons:
         Le'ê'ad, 'Anaq, Sabkê, Yeter; and two daughters: Zezekô,
         Lezek.

1.15-17 Enoch fathered, after Methuselah (see Gen 5.21-22), five
         sons: 'Ănaz, Lê'ôn, 'Akawôn, P^{e}lêdî, 'Elêd; and three daugh-
         ters: Tê'îz, Lêpîd, La'ê'ad. And the Lord found delight
         in Enoch and took him away (see Gen 5.24).

1.18-19 Methuselah (fathered),[7] after Lamech (see Gen 5.28-29), two
         sons and two daughters: 'Inab, Rapô', 'Alûmāh, 'Amûgah.

1.20   *And Lamech fathered Noah saying: This one will comfort us*
         and give rest[8] *to the earth and to everyone who is on it,*
         for the Lord will visit evil upon the earth because of the
         violence which is in the evildoers.

[*LAB* 1.21 says that Lamech lived 585 years after Noah's birth (Gen
5.30).]

---

[8]The reading יְנַחֲמֵנוּ is MT, but *LAB* has *requiem dabit nobis* (=
LXX?; διαναπαύσει ἡμᾶς). *CJ* appears to offer both MT and LXX readings.

רנח הוליד ג֗ בנים שם רחם ויפת: 10

רישב קין ואשתו תֵּמָד בארץ נד: 11

וידע קין את אֶשֶׁתוֹ תֵּמָד   =2.2

בן עֹ֗ שנה ותולד את חנוך ויבן שבעה עיירות ויקרא הראשונה כשם   =2.3
בנו חנוך .... מָאוּלִי לֵיאָד גֵּיזָה יֶשָׁכַה קֶלָר יֵיבַב:

ויולד קין אחרי חנוך ג֗ בנים אגֵּלָף לֵינָף פ֗ג֗ל רֹב֗ בנות צִיטַא ומַחַת: 12

ויקח חנוך את נָיבָא בת שם לאשה ותלד לו את זֵירָא ואת קג֗עית ואת   13
מַבַּף וזיירא הוליד את מתושאל ומתושאל את למך:

ויקח למך ב֗ נשים: 14

עדה ילדה יובל אבי כל ירשב אהל (ר)מקנה ואת יבל אבי כל תופש   =2.7
כינור ועוגב:

אז החלו יושבי הארץ לעשות החמס לטמא איש את אשת רעהו לחרות אף   15
יי ויחל לזמר בכינור ועוגב ולשחוק בכל מיני זמר לשחת הארץ:

[*CJ* 26.15-20 continues with descriptions of Jubal's contributions to
the science of music, Tubalcain's inventions for working with metals,
and Jabal's devices for safeguarding flocks and tents as well as information about Enoch's assumption.]

ויהי המבול ויצא נח מן התיבה ויעל עולות וירח יי ויאמר לא אוסיף   21
עוד לקלל ולהכות את כל חי כי כי אם כאשר יחטאו אשפטם ברעב ובחרב
ובאש ובדבר וברעש ואפיצם הנה והנה: ואזכור זאת ליושב(י) הארץ
עד עת קץ:

---

[9]Some such addition must be made.

[10]As in *LAB*, the Mehujael generation is omitted. Also, the
author has read זֵירָד rather than the MT עִירָד.

[11]The Hebrew does not correspond exactly to the MT here and in
the preceding verse.

[12]A *waw* must be inserted (see the biblical text).

[13]The two names have been reversed in relation to their biblical sequence.

[14]The biblical sequence of words is not followed.

[15]In the light of the context and *LAB* (*qui inhabitant terram*)
a plural reading is necessary.

1.22   And *Noah* fathered three sons: *Shem and Ham and Japhet*
        (Gen 5.32).

2.1   *And Cain* and his wife Tēmēd *dwelt in the land of Nod* (Gen
        4.16).

2.2   *And Cain knew his wife* (Gen 4.17) Tēmēd

2.3   when he was 15 years old, and she bore Enoch; and he built
        seven cities, *and he named* the first *according to the name
        of his son Enoch* (Gen 4.17). (The names of the others
        were:)[9] Ma'ôlî, Lê'ed, Gêzeh, Yeškah, Qeler, Yêbab.

2.4   And Cain fathered, after Enoch, three sons: 'Ûlap, Lêzup,
        Pûzal; and two daughters: Sêṭa' and Maḥat.

2.5   And Enoch took Nîba', the daughter of Shem, for a wife; and
        she bore to him Zêra' and Qû'ît and Maddap. And Zêra'
        fathered Methushael,[10] and Methushael Lamech (see Gen 4.18).

2.6   *And Lamech took* two *wives* (Gen 4.19).

2.7   Adah bore Yûbal,[11] *the father of* everyone *dwelling in tents
        (and having)*[12] *cattle, and* Yabal,[13] *the father of everyone
        playing the lyre and pipe* (Gen 4.20-21).

2.8   Then the inhabitants of the earth began to do violence, to
        defile each man the wife of his neighbor, to kindle the
        anger of the Lord; and he began to play on the lyre and
        pipe and to make sport with all kinds of song, to corrupt
        the earth.

[*LAB* 2.9-3.8 records the birth of Tubal, the lament of Lamech, the
reason for the flood and the instructions to Noah, and finally the
story of the flood itself ending with the building of an altar.]

3.9   And the flood took place, and Noah went forth from the ark
        and offered holocausts. And the Lord smelled (them) and
        said: "*I will never again curse*[14] (Gen 8.20-22) and smite
        every living thing; but, when they will sin, I will judge
        them with famine and with the sword and with fire and with
        pestilence and with earthquake, and I shall scatter them
        here and there. And I will remember this for the inhabi-
        tant(s)[15] of the earth until the time of the end.

3.10= ריהי במלאת קץ העולם וידום האור רת‹כב›ה החשך ואחיה את המתים

ואקיץ ישיני האדמה: וישיב השאול את חובו והאבדון ישיב חלקו

ואשיב לרשע כפרי מעלליו ואשפוט בין בשר לנפש: רינוח בהשקט העולם

ובלע המות לנצח ושאול תסכר את פיה: ולא יהיה עוד הארץ בלי צמח

ולא יעקרו יושביה ולא יטמאוה המשפטים כי הארץ חדשה ושמים חדשים

יהיו לישיבת עולם:

---

[16]The MS has חבכה ("will weep"), but in view of *LAB*'s *et ex-
tinguentur tenebre* תכבה would be correct. While I am not sure how
the darkness can be extinguished, the context and parallelism implies
that *LAB* and our emendation are more correct than *CJ*.

[17]For יעקרו Gaster has "be rooted out" while *LAB* has *sterilis*;
LAB's interpretation has been followed in the translation.

3.10   And it will happen when the appointed time of the world is
        fulfilled that the light will cease and the darkness will
        ⟨be extinguished⟩[16] and I will resurrect the dead and arouse
        those sleeping in the ground, and Sheol will repay its debt
        and Abaddon will repay its portion, and I will repay the
        wicked man according to the fruit of his deeds, and I will
        judge between flesh and soul. And the world will rest in
        silence, and death will be swallowed up forever (see 1 Cor
        15.54; Isa 25.8), and Sheol will shut its mouth. And the
        earth will no more be without growth, and its inhabitants
        will not be sterile ,[17] and those judged guilty[18] will not
        defile it, for the new earth and the new heaven will be an
        everlasting habitation.

[*LAB* 3.11-4.1 describes the covenant with Noah and the promise of
the bow, and begins the genealogy by listing the three sons of Noah.]

---

[18]As the text stands, we would translate: "the judgments will
not defile it"; we should probably emend to הנשפטים (suggested by
Michael Stone), as our translation implies. *LAB* has *et non coin-
quinabitur ullus qui in me iustificatus est.*

27.1 בני יפת גומר   ומגוג מדי ריון ותובל משך ותירס: ובני גומר
אשכנז וריפת ותוגרמה: ובני ירן אלישה ותרשיש כתים ודודנים:

2   בני גומר מֶלֶד לוד דֶבֶר בַלַד: בני מגוג קַשָּׁא טִיפָא פַרהִטַא עמיאל
פנחס גוֹלַאזַא סַמַבָך: בני דדן שלוס פִּילוֹג טורפליטא: בני תובל
פאנטורניא אטיפא: בני תירס מאך טבאל בלענה שמפלא מִיַאה אִילַש:
בני מלך אבורדד הורד בוצרה: בני אשכנז וכל סַרדַנַא אַבַך: בני
יַעירִי הֶרִי אִיצוֹגדַד דוֹעַט דְיִפַסִיַאת חנוך: בני תוגרמה אביהוד שפט
זיפטיר: בני אלישה זעק קנת מסטידרידא: בני זיפתי מפשיאל טינא
ארולא איאינוך: בני טיסי מָקוֹל לוּאוֹן צֶלַגטַבַג: בני דודנים אִיטַב
בִיַאת ופֶגֶג:

=4.3   מאלה נפרדו יושבי ארץ פרס ומדי ואיי הים:

3   וייעל פנג בן דודנים ויחל להיות ספן באניות הים: אז נפצה שליש
ארץ

=4.4   רומירת: ויכבשו בניו את ידיד: ובני מגוג כבשו להם את דִיגֶל ובני
מדי כבשו את בְטָטוֹ ובני יון כבשו את צָאֶל ובני תובל כבשו את פחח
ובני משך כבשו את גֶפְטִי: ובני תירס כבשו את רואו ובני דינים
כבשו את גוֹדָה וריפת בלא בניו כבש את גוֹדוֹ ובני ריפת כבשו את
בוצרה: ובני תוגרמה כבשו את פוט: בני אלישה כבשו את טבלו ובני
תרשיש את מריבא: ובני כתים ....:   ובני דודנים את קַרוּבַא:

=4.5   ואז החלו לעבוד את האדמה וכאשר צמאה למים ויקראו אל יי וירויה
מטר: ויהי ברדת הגשם ונראה הקשת בענן ויראו יושבי הארץ את אות
הברית ויברכו את יי:

---

[1]Dedan stands in place of Madi or Javan; one of these has been omitted.

[2]The name should be משך rather than מלך in the light of Gen 10.2. Also this line should precede the "sons of Tiras."

[3]'Êrî/Herî should be Riphath. 'Êrî is probably a false reading corrected with the following Herî.

[4]Mastîdrîda' in *LAB* is two names--Mastisa (or Mastifa) and Rira.

[5]Zêptî must be Kittim.

[6]Têsî must be Tarshish. The order of this and the preceding lines has been reversed.

[7]*LAB* here has *Domereth et filii eius* which clearly should be *Gomer et filii eius*. The error, which is most explicable in Latin, has been compounded by the Hebrew retroverter. See the introduction.

[8]For Dînîm *LAB* has Duodenin; in fact, both *CJ* and *LAB* should

4.2   *The sons of Japhet: Gomer and Magog, Madai and Javan and*
       Tubal, Meshech and Tiras. And the sons of Gomer: Ashkenaz,
       and Riphath and Togarmah. And the sons of Javan: Elishah
       and Tarshish, Kittim and Dodanim (Gen 10.2-4).

       The sons of Gomer: Ṭeled, Lûd, Deber and Led.

       The sons of Magog: Qaše', Ṭîpa', Parûta', ʿAmî'el, Pinḥas,
       Gôla'aza', Samanāk.

       The sons of Dedan:[1] Šalûs, Pîlôg, Ṭûplîṭa.

       The sons of Tubal: Pa'anṭônya', 'Eṭîpa'.

       The sons of Tiras: Ma'ak, Ṭab'el, Bal'anah, Šampla', Mê'ah,
       'Êlaš.

       The sons of Melek:[2] 'Abûradad, Hûrad, Bôṣarah.

       The sons of Ashkenaz: Vekal, Sardana', 'Anak.

       The sons of ⌜Êrî⌝ Herî:[3] 'Eṣûdad, Dô'at, Dêpasê'at, Ḥanôk.

       The sons of Togarmah: 'Abîhûd, Šapaṭ, Zêpṭîr.

       The sons of Elishah: Za'aq, Qenat, Masṭîdrîda'.[4]

       The sons of Zêptî:[5] Mapšî'el, Ṭêna', 'Aula', 'Î'înôn.

       The sons of Ṭêsî:[6] Māqôl, Lû'ôn, Ṣilagtābag.

       The sons of Dodanim: 'Îṭeb, Bê'at, and Paneg.

4.3   *From these were spread abroad* (Gen 10.5) the inhabitants of
       the land of Persia and Media and the islands of the sea.
       And Paneg, the son of Dodanim, went up and began to sail in
       the boats of the sea. Then a third of the land of Rômêret[7]
       was separated off.

4.4   And his sons conquered Yadêd, and the sons of Magog conquered
       for themselves Dêgel, and the sons of Madai conquered Biṭṭô,
       and the sons of Javan conquered Ṣe'el, and the sons of Tubal
       conquered Paḥat, and the sons of Meshech conquered Nepṭî, and
       the sons of Tiras conquered Rô'ô, and the sons of Dînîm[8] con-
       quered Gôdah, and Riphath without his sons conquered Gôdô, and
       the sons of Riphath conquered Bôṣorah, and the sons of Togar-
       mah conquered Pûṭ, and the sons of Elishah conquered Ṭablô,
       and the sons of Tarshish Merîba', and the sons of Kittim....,[9]
       and the sons of Dodanim Qarûba'.

4.5   And then they began to work the land; and when it thirsted
       for water, then they cried to the Lord and he soaked it by rain.
       And when the rain descended, the bow appeared in the cloud
       and the inhabitants of the earth saw the sign of the covenant
       and blessed the Lord.

---

have Ashekanaz.

[9]Here *LAB* has *Cethim et filii eius acceperunt Thaan.*

4   רבני חם כוש ומצרי ופוט וכנען: ואלה בני כוש שבא .... וטודן:
ובני מאיפון טינוש ציליור טִילוף גילוג ליפוך: ובני כנען צידון
ואנדאים רצין שימים אורואין נימיגים חמתים ניפים טילש אילג כושים:

4.7=   וכוש ילד את נמרוד הוא החל להיות נפיל גאה לפני יי: ומצרים ילד
את לודים ואת ענמים ואת להבים ואת נפתוחים ופתרוסים וכסלוחים
וכפתורים:

4.8=   והם החלו לבנות עיירות אלה צידון ובנותיה ריסון ביאוזא מזאגר
תשקלון דבר קמו טילון לאכיש סדום ועמורה אדמה וצבוים:

5   ובני שם עילם ואשור וארפכשד ולוד וארן: ובני אשור גזרון ישי:
וארפכשד ילד את שלח ושלח ילד את עבר: ולעבר יולד שני בנים שם
האחד פלג כי בימיו נפלגה הארץ ושם אחיו יקטן:

4.10=   ויקטן ילד את אלמודד ואת שלפטרא ואת מוזאם וריאדורא ועוזים
דיקלבל מימואל שַבְיטחָפִין חזילה יובב: ובני פלג רעו ריפוד שפרה
אקולון זכר זיפך גבי שורי שזיאור פלאבוש רפא פלטיא שפדיפל שייש
והרטמן אליפז: אלה בני פלג ואלה שמותם ויקחו להם נשים מבנות
יקטן ויולדו בנים ובנות ותמלא הארץ מהם:

6   ויקח לו רעו את מלכה בת רות לאשה ויולד את שרוג וימלאו ימיה ללדת
ויאמר רעו: מזה יצא עד דור רביעי אשר יותן כסאו עליה ויקרא תמים
צדיק ואב המון גוים: לא יעזבו עדותו וימלאו זרעו את העולם:

4.12=   ויולד רעו אחרי שרוג ז בנים אביאל עובד שלמא דידזל קניזא עכור
נפש רה בנות קדימא דריפא שאיפא פיריטא תהילה:

---

[10]As in *LAB*, there is a lacuna in Gen 10.7:   Seba (Havilah,
Sabtah, Raamah and Sabteca. The sons of Raamah: Sheba) and Dedan.
As in *LAB*, טודן has been misread for דדן.

[11]*CJ* (against *LAB*) omits from Gen 10.14 the phrase "whence came
the Philistines."

[12]For Bê'ôza', Mazagar, Yaśqalôn, Dabir, Qamô *LAB* has *Beosamaza*
(or *Beosomata*), *Geras, Calon, Dabircamo.*

[13]In this place in Gen 10.23 we would expect "The sons of Aram:
Uz, Hul, Gether, and Mash." *LAB* is very corrupt here also: *filiarum*
(some MSS *filirum*) *Assum Gedrumese* (some MSS *Gredu Messe*).

[14]The MT of Gen 10.26-29 yields "Sheleph, Hazarmaveth, Jerah,
Hadoram, Uzal, Diklah, Obal, Abimael, Sheba, Ophir, Havilah, and
Jobab." *LAB* is very corrupt here: *Salastra, Mazaam* (or *Muzaam*),
Rea, Dura, Uzia (or *Ream, Duram, Uziam*), *Deglabal, Mimoel, Sabthfin*
(or *Sabthifin*), *Evilach, Iubab.*

4.6   *And the sons of Ham: Cush, and Egypt, and Put and Canaan.*
And these are *the sons of Cush* (Gen 10.6-7): Šeba....[10] and
Ṭûdan. And the sons of Ma'îpûn: Ṭînûš, Ṣêlêwû, Tîlûp, Gêlûg,
Lêpûk.
And the sons of Canaan: Sidon and 'Anda'îm, Raṣîn, Šimîm,
'Ûrû'în, Nêmîgîm, Ḥamatîm, Nêfîm, Ṭêlaš, 'Êlag, Cûšîm (see
Gen 10.15-18).

4.7   *And Cush fathered Nimrod; he began to be* a proud giant
before the Lord (Gen 10.8-9). *And Egypt begat the Ludim and
Anamim and Lehabim and Naphtuhim and Pathrusim and Casluhim
and*[11] *Caphtorim* (Gen 10.13-14).

4.8   And they began to build cities. These (were) *Sidon* and its
daughter villages, Rêsûn, Bê'ôza', Mazagar, Yašqalôn, Dabir,
Qamô,[12] Ṭêlûn, La'kîš, *Sodom and Gomorrah, Admah and Zeboiim*
(Gen 10.19).

4.9   *And the sons of Shem: Elam and Asshur and Arpachshad and Lud
and Aran.*
And the sons of Asshur: Gezrôn, Yišî.[13] *And Arpachshad
fathered Shelah, and Shelah fathered Eber; and to Eber were
born two sons, the name of the one was Peleg, for in his days
the earth was divided, and the name of his brother was Joktan*
(Gen 10.22-25).

4.10   *And Joktan fathered Almodad and* (Gen 10.26) Šalaptra' and
Mûza'am and Rê'adûra' and 'Ûzîm, Dêqlabal, Mîmô'el, Šabêṭṭ[e]pîn,
Hazilah, Jobab[14] (see Gen 10.26-29).
And the sons of Peleg: Reu, Rêpûd, Šeparah, 'Aqûlôn, Zakar,
Zîpak, Gabî, Šûrî, Šezî'ûr, Pala'buš, Rafo', Palṭîa', Šapdêpal,
Šayîš and Harṭeman, 'Elîpaz. And these are the *sons of Peleg*
(see Gen 11.17-19), and these are their names. And they took
for themselves wives from the daughters of Joktan; and sons
and daughters were born, and the earth was filled by them.

4.11   And Reu took for himself Melkah the daughter of Ruth for a
wife, and he begat Serug. And her days to bear were fulfilled,
and Reu said: "From this one there will issue in the fourth
generation he whose throne will be raised high, and he will
be called 'perfect, just and father of a host of nations.' And
the promises made to him will not be abandoned, and his seed
will fill the world."

4.12   And Reu fathered, after Serug (see Gen 11.21), seven sons:
Abî'el, 'Ôbed, Šalma', Dêdazal, Qenêza, 'Akûr, Nepeš; and
five daughters: Qedêma', Derîpa', Še'îpa, Pêrîta', Tehîlah.

4.13=   וייולד שרוג אחרי נחור ד בנים צילה דיגא סובא ופורא וג בנות גיזלא חוגלה שליפא:

7   וייולד נחור אחרי תרח ו בנים רכב דדיאב בריכב ושיבל שף נידב קמואל וח בנות יסכה טיפא ברונא קניטא: ויקח את אמתלאי בת כרנבו:

8   ויחי תרח ע שנח וייולד את אברם ואת נחור ואת הרן והרן הוליד את לוט:

9   אז החלו יושבי הארץ לראות במזלות ולהיות חוזים בכוכבים ולקסום כקסמים והיו נותנים בניהם ובנותיהם באש ושרוג ובניו לא הלכו בדרכ‹ה›ם:

---

[15]The order in *LAB Zoba, Dica* is reversed in *CJ*.

[16]The *LAB* MSS K and P (Fulda-Cassel Theol. 4°3 and Phillipps 461) which are usually the best have *Recap, Dediap, Berechap* while the others have *Recab, Dediab, Berechab*. In *LAB* Nahor is said to have eight sons, and eight are named; in *CJ* he has six sons, and seven are named.

[17]*LAB* has *Cene, Etha*; also Nahor is said to have five daughters, and five are named. In *CJ* he has eight daughters, but only four

4.13   And Serug fathered, after Nahor (see Gen 11.22-23), four sons:
        Sêlah, Dîga', Sôba' [15] and Pôra'; and three daughters:
        Gêzila', Ḥôglah, Šelîpa'.

4.14   And Nahor fathered, after Terah (Gen 11.24-25), six sons:
        Recab, Dedî'ab, Berêkab,[16] and Šîbal, Šap, Nîdab, Qamô'el;
        and eight daughters: Yeskah, Ṭîpa', Bᵉrûna', Qanêṭa'.[17] And
        he took 'Amtalaî the daughter of Karnabô.[18]

4.15   *And Terah lived 70 years and fathered Abram and Nahor and
        Haran; and Haran fathered Lot* (Gen 11.26-27).

4.16   Then the inhabitants of the earth began to divine by constel-
        lations and to be gazers by the stars and to practice divina-
        tion like the diviners, and they were making their sons and
        daughters pass through the fire. But Serug and his sons did
        not walk in ⟨their⟩ ways.[19]

---

are named.

[18]The sentence has no parallel in *LAB*.

[19]The MS has בדרכיכם; the emendation to בדרכיהם is based on the
context and *LAB*'s *non ambulaverunt secundum eos*.

28.1 ואלה תולדות נח בארצותם למשפחותם ללשונותם ונפוצו כגרייהם בארץ
אחר המבול:

5.1= ריבואר בני חם וישימו עליהם את נמרוד לשר ולנגיד וגם בני יפת
נתנו עליהם את פנחס לשר ולנגיד וגם בני שם נתנו עליהם את יקטן
לשר ולנגיד:

2 ריבואו שלשת הנגידים האלה ויועצו יחדיו לקרב את עסם אליהם כעוד
נח אביהם חי ויקרבו כל העם אליהם ויהיו לנפש אחד ריהי השלום בארץ:

3 ריהי בשנת שש מאות וארבעים שנה לצאת נח מן התיבה ויפקד כל נגיד
את בני עמו:

5.4= ויפקד פנחס את בני יפת ובני גומר ויהיו כל פקודי פנחס חמשת אלפים
ושמנה מאות: ומבני מגוג אשר תחת ידו ששת אלפים ומאתים: ומבני
מדי תחת ידו חמשת אלפים ושבע מאות: בני תובל תחת ידו תשעת אלפים
וארבע מאות: ובני משך שבעת אלפים ומאתים: בני תירס שנים עשר אלף
ושלש מאות: בני ריפת אחד עשר אלף וחמש מאות: בני תוגרמה ארבעה
עשר אלף וארבע מאות: בני אלישה ארבעה עשר אלף ותשע מאות: בני
תרשיש שנים עשר אלף ומאה: בני כתים שמנה עשר אלף ושלש מאות: בני
דודנים שבעה עשר אלף ושבע מאות: ויהיו כל פקודי בני יפת אנשי חיל
נושאי כלי מלחמה כאשר פנחס נשיא שלהם פקדם מאה וארבעים ושתים
אלפים לבד מן הנשים והטף:

4 גם נמרוד הנשיא העביר את בני חם תחת שבטו רימצאם שנים עשר אלף ושש
מאות: בני מצרים תחת ידו עשרים וארבעה אלף ותשע מאות: ובני פוט
עשרים ושבעה אלף ושבע מאות: ובני כנען שנים ושלשים אלף ותשע
מאות: בני שבא ארבעת אלפים ושלש מאות: בני חוילה ארבעה ועשרים

---

[1] *LAB* has 340.

[2] Where *CJ* has תחת ידו, *LAB* transeuntes secundum sceptra ducationis sue; see the Introduction for a discussion of the passage.

[3] Javan is absent, as in *LAB*.

[4] *LAB* has 5600.

[5] Ashkenaz is absent, as in *LAB*.

[6] *LAB* has 17300.

[7] Cush is absent, as in *LAB*.

[8] *LAB* has 24800.

[9] The best *LAB* MSS (KP) have 32800 while the others have 32900.

4.17   And these are the generations of Noah *in their lands accord-*
       ing to their tribes according to their tongues; and they were
       scattered according to their nations *on the earth after the*
       flood (Gen 10.31-32).

5.1   And the sons of Ham came and set over themselves Nimrod as
       prince and chief; and also the sons of Japhet placed over
       themselves Pinḥas as prince and chief; and also the sons of
       Shem placed over themselves Joktan as prince and chief.

5.2   And these three chiefs came and took counsel together to
       bring their people near to them while Noah their father was
       still alive; and all the people drew near to them. And they
       were of one soul, and there was peace on earth.

5.3   And it happened that, 640 years[1] after Noah went forth from
       the ark, every chief numbered the sons of his people.

5.4   And Pinḥas numbered the sons of Japhet and the sons of Gomer
       (see Gen 10.2-4).
       And all those numbered by Pinḥas were 5800.
       And from the sons of Magog who were beneath his hand[2] 6200.
       And from the sons of Madai beneath his hand 5700.[3]
       The sons of Tubal beneath his hand 9400.
       And the sons of Meshech 7200.[4]
       The sons of Tiras 12300.[5]
       The sons of Riphath 11500.
       The sons of Togarmah 14400.
       The sons of Elishah 14900.
       The sons of Tarshish 12100.
       The sons of Kittim 18300.[6]
       The sons of Dodanim 17700.
       And all those numbered of the sons of Japhet, men of valor,
       bearers of the arms of war, when Pinḥas their leader numbered
       them, were 142000 apart from women and children.

5.5   Also Nimrod the leader made the sons of Ham (see Gen 10.6-7)
       pass beneath his staff and found them to be 12600.[7]
       The sons of Egypt beneath his hand 24900.[8]
       And the sons of Puṭ 27700.
       And the sons of Canaan 32900.[9]
       The sons of Seba 4300.[10]

_____

[10]The number is the same as that of *LAB*, but in both cases it
is disproportionately small.

אלף רשלש מאות: בני סבתא חמשה ועשרים אלף ושלש מאות: ובני רעמה

שלשים אלף רשש מאות: בני סבתכא ששה וארבעים אלף וארבע מאות:

ויהיו כל פקודי בני הם כאשר נמרוד הנשיא פקד אותם תשעה וארבעים

אלף ומאתים אלף אנשי חיל יוצאי צבא לבד מן הנשים והטף:

5   ויהיו כל פקודי בני נח ארבעה עשר אלף ושבע מאות אלפים ומאה: כל

אלה התפקדו בעוד נח חי ויחי נח אחרי המבול שלש מאות שנה וחמישים

שנה: ויהיו כל ימי נח תשע מאות שנה וחמשים שנה וימות:

---

[11]Here *LAB* KP have the 46400 with *CJ* while the others have 36400.
[12]*LAB* has 244900.
[13]The census of the sons of Shem, present in *LAB* 5.6--7, is absent from *CJ*.

The sons of Havilah 24300.

The sons of Sabtah 25300.

The sons of Raamah 30600.

The sons of Sabteca 46400.[11]

And all those numbered of the sons of Ham when Nimrod the leader numbered them were 249000,[12] men of valor going out to war, apart from women and children.[13]

[*LAB* 5.6-7 records the census of the sons of Shem by Joktan.]

5.8   And all those numbered of the sons of Noah were 714100.[14]

And all these were numbered while Noah was still alive. *And Noah lived after the flood 350 years. And all the days of Noah were 950 years, and he died* (Gen 9.28-39).

---

[14]*LAB* has 814100.

29.1 ויהי כאשר נפרדו יושבי הארץ ויקהלו יחדיו ויסעו מקדם וימצאו בקעה
      בארץ בבל וישבו שם: ויאמרו איש אל רעהו הנה בא העת אשר נפוץ איש
      מאת רעהו באחרית הימים ואיש באחיר וילחם לנו: הבה נבנה לנו עיר
      ומגדל וראשו בשמים ונעשה לנו שם גדול על הארץ:

2   ויאמרו איש אל רעהו הבה נלבנה לבינים ויכתב כל איש את שמו
      ב{י}לבינתו ונשרפה לשרפה ותהי לנו הלבינה לאבן וההחמר יהיה לנו
      לחמר:

=6.3 ויעש כל איש לבינתו ויכתב את שמו עליה מלבד שנים עשר א<נש>ים
      אשר לא רצו להיות עמהם:

3   ואלה שמות האנשים אשר לא היו בעצתם אברם נחור לוט רעו טינוטי צבא
      אלמודד יובב אצר אבימאל שבא אופיר:

=6.4 ויקחו אותם עם הארץ ויביאום אל נשיאיהם ויאמרו אלה האנשים אשר
      עברו על העיצה אשר יעצנו כי לא רצו ללכת בדרכינו:

4   ויאמרו להם הנשיאים למה לא חפצתם לעשות הלבינים עם עמי הארץ
      ויענו להם ויאמרו לא נעשה הלבינים ולא נדבק בכם כי אל אחד ידענו
      ואותו נעבד אף כי הייתם שורפים אותנו באש עם הלבינים לא נלך
      בדרכיכם:

5   ויחר לנשיאים ויאמרו כאשר דברו כן נעשה להם כי אם לא יעשו כמונו
      תשימו אותם באש על<ם> לביניכם:

6   ויען יקטן ראש הנשיאים ויאמר לא כן נעשה כי אם נתן להם זמן שבעת
      ימים והיה אם יחפצו לעשות עמכם חלביניכם יחיר ואם לא יחפצו ימותו
      באש כי בקש להצילם מידם כי ראש לבית אבותם הוא ואף כי עבדו את יי:

=6.7 ויעשו כן ויתנום בבית הסהר בית יקטן:

---

[1]Either וילחם is to be understood as stative (as Gaster did) or
emendation is necessary. *LAB* has for this *and* the preceding *alteru-
trum erimus expugnantes nos.* Perhaps read לו for לנו (M. Stone).

[2]There is an intrusive *yodh* between ב and ל in the MS form.

[3]The MS has אלפים; the emendation to אנשים is obviously correct
from sense and *LAB extra viros duodecim.*

[4]The first four names are clear enough. For Almôdad, Yôbab,
'Abîma'el, Šaba' and 'Ôpîr, compare Gen 10.26-29. The remaining
names in *LAB* are *Tenute, Zaba* and *Esar* as in *CJ.*

[5]עם is read for MS על in the light of the above phrase עם הלבינים
and *LAB cum lapidibus vestris.*

6.1   And when the inhabitants of the earth had been spread abroad,
        they gathered together and journeyed *from the east and found*
        a plain in the land of Babel *and settled there. And they*
        said, each man to his neighbor (Gen 11.2-3): "Behold the
        time is coming when we will be scattered, each man from his
        neighbor, at the end of days; and each man will be against
        his brother, and there will be war[1] for us. *Come, let us*
        build for ourselves a city and a tower, and its top will be
        in the heavens; and we will make for ourselves a great name
        (Gen 11.4) upon the earth."

6.2   *And they said, each man to his neighbor: "Come, let us make*
        bricks; and each man will write his name on his brick;[2] *and*
        let us burn them thoroughly. And the brick will be for us
        for stone, and the pitch will be for us *for mortar* (Gen 11.3).

6.3   And every man made his own brick and wrote his name on it ex-
        cept for twelve ⟨men⟩[3] who did not wish to be with them.
        And these were the names of the men who were not in their
        plan: Abram, Nahor, Lot, Reu, Ṭênûṭê, Ṣaba', 'Almôdad, Yôbab,
        'Eṣar, 'Abîma'el, Šaba', 'Ôpîr[4] (see Gen 10.26-29).

6.4   And the people of the land took them and brought them to their
        leaders, and they said: "These are the men who rejected the
        plan which we planned, for they do not wish to walk in our
        ways."
        And the leaders said to them: "Why are you not willing to
        make bricks along with the peoples of the land?" And they
        answered them and said: "We will not make bricks and we will
        not join with you, for the one God we know and him we serve.
        Even if you burn us in the fire along with the bricks, we will
        not walk in your ways."

6.5   And this angered the leaders, and they said: "As they said,
        thus we will do to them; for, if they do not do as we do, you
        will cast them in the fire ⟨with⟩[5] your bricks."

6.6   And Joktan the head of the leaders answered and said: "We
        will not act in this way, but we will give them the period of
        seven days. And if they are willing to make bricks with you,
        they will live; and if they are not willing, they will die in
        the fire." For he sought to rescue them from their hand,
        because he was head of the house of their fathers and because
        they served the Lord.[6]

---

[6]*LAB* has: *quoniam de tribu erat et Deo serviebat.*

7   ויהי בערב ויצו ויקטן הנשיא לחמשים איש גבורי חיל ויאמר להם
התאזרו וקחו לי האנשים הלילה האסורים בביתי ושימו אותם על עשר
פרדים וגם צדה להם ולגמלים והביאום אל ההרים ותחיר עמהם שם והיה
אם תגידו את הדבר הזה באש תשרפו:

8   וילכו האנשים ויעשו כן ויקחום לילה ויביאום לפני יקטן הנשיא:

6.9=   ויאמר להם אתם הדבקים ביי בטחו בו עדי כי הוא יציל אתכם
ויושיע אתכם: לכן הנה צויתי לחמשים האנשים האלה להביאכם אל
ההרים וגם צדה לכם לאכלה ונחבאתם שם אל הבקעות כי מים בבקעה
לש⟨ב⟩עות עד מלאת שלשים יום כי אז יעבור לב עם הארץ מעליכם או
יחרה אף יי בעם וישחית אותם כי ידעתי כי לא יילינו בעצתם הרעה אשר
{י}זמר לעשות כי און מחשבותם:

9   והיה לשבעת הימים כאשר יבקשר אתכם ואומר להם כי שברו את פתח בית
הכלא ויצאו וברחו בלילה ושלחתי מאה לרדוף אחריהם ולבקשם וכל זאת
אעשה לשכך חמחם מכם:

6.10=   ויענו האחד עשר אנשים ויאמרו לו הנה מצאנו חן בעיניך כי הצלת את
נפשותינו מיד אויבינו:

10   ויחריש אברם לבדו ויאמר לו יקטן הנשיא למה לא ענית לי דבר עם רעיך
ויען אברם ויאמר הנה אנחנו בורחים היום אל ההרים להמלט מן האש
ואם יצאו מן ההרים חיות רעות יאכלונו או אם יחסר לנו מאכל ונמות
ברעב נמצאנו בורחים לפני עם הארץ ונמות בחטאתינו: ועתה חי יי
אשר בטחתי בו כי לא אמיש מן המקום אשר כלאוני כן והיה אם יש בי
עון אשר אמות בו אמות כרצון יי אשר ירצה:

_____

[7]CJ's text is simpler than *LAB*, but *LAB* makes no mention of
camels as *CJ* does.
[8]Gaster's translation implies emending MS לשעות to לשבעות;
לשתות ("to drink") is also possible.
[9]The MS has the imperfect יזמו, but the perfect זמר seems in
order. *LAB* has *consiliati sunt*.

6.7   And thus they did, and they put them in the jail at Joktan's
house.
And it happened in the evening that Joktan the leader commanded fifty mighty men of valor and said to them:
"Gird yourselves, and take for me this night the men imprisoned in my house, and put them on ten mules and also food for
them and for the camels.[7] And bring them to the mountains,
and stay with them there. And it will happen that, if you
tell of this matter, you will be burned in the fire."

6.8   And the men went and did thus. And they took them by night
and brought them before Joktan the leader.

6.9   And he said to them: "You who cling to the Lord, trust in
him forever, for he will rescue you and save you. Therefore,
behold I have commanded these fifty men to bring you to the
mountains and also food for you for eating. And you will be
hidden there in the valleys, for in the valley there is ⟨suf-
ficient⟩[8] water until the end of thirty days; for then the
heart of the people of the land will turn from you or the
anger of the Lord will be kindled against the people and he
will destroy them; for I know that they will not abide in
their evil plan which they have devised[9] to do because their
plots are wicked.
And at the end of seven days when they seek you, I will say
to them that 'they broke down the door of the prison and went
forth and fled by night. And I sent 100 men to pursue them
and to seek them out.' And all this I will do to abate their
wrath from you."

6.10   And the eleven men answered and said to him: "Behold we have
found favor in your eyes, for you have rescued our lives from
the hand of our enemies."

6.11   But Abram alone was silent, and Joktan the leader said to him:
"Why have you not answered me a word along with your companions?" Abram answered and said: "Behold we are fleeing
today to the mountains to escape from the fire. And if wild
beasts go forth from the mountains, they will devour us. Or
if we lack food, then we will die by famine. We will be
fleeing before the people of the land, and we will die in our
sins. And now as the Lord lives in whom I have trusted, I
will not move from the place in which they have imprisoned
me. And if there is any iniquity in me for which I should
die, I will die according to the will of the Lord as he wills."

11   ויאמר לו הנשיא דמך בראשך אם לא תברח עם האנשים האלה כי אם תברח

        תינצל ויאמר אברם לא אברח כי אם אשאר:

6.12=   ויקחו את אברם ויתנ‹ו›הו בית הכלא וישלח הנשיא את האחד עשר

        אנשים ביד חמשים איש אל ההרים וגם צדה שלח להם בעשרה גמלים ביד

        חמשים אחרים ויצו להם להיות עמהם עד חמשה עשר יום ולשוב לאמר לא

        מצאנום ואם לא תעשו כן אשרוף אתכם באש:

12   ויהי לשבעת ימים ויקהלו כל העם ויאמרו אל נשיאיהם תנו לנו את

        האנשים אשר לא רצו להיות בעצתינו ונשרפם באש וישלחו להביאם ולא

        נמצאו כי אם אברם:

6.14=   ויאמרו פנחס ונמרוד הנשיאים אל יקטן הנשיא איה האנשים האסורים

        בבית הסהר בביתך ויאמר להם יקטן הנה שברו הלילה ויצאו ושלחתי

        אחריהם מאה אנשים לבקשם ולהמיתם:

6.15=   ויאמרו כל העם הנה לא מצאנו כי אם אברם נשרפהו באש:

13   ויקחו את אברם ויעמידהו לפני הנשיאים וישאלוהו לאמר איה האנשים

        אשר סגרנו עמך ויאמר אברם לא ידעתי כי ישנתי הלילה וכאשר הקיצותי

        לא מצאתים:

6.16=   ויעשר תנור כבשן ויחממוהו עד יקוד אש עם לבינה 'אברם ויתנוהו

        ע‹ם› הלבינה בכבשן האש וישכך יקטן את חמת כל העם בשריפת אברם:

14   רייי הרעיש רעש גדול בכל הארץ ותצא האש מן הכבשן ויהי ללהבה ותאכל

        את כל האנשים אשר סביבות הכבשן ויהי מספר הנשרפים ביום ההוא

        ארבעה ושמונים אלף וחמש מאות ואברם לא נשרף מן האש:

6.18=   ויצא מן הכבשן מאור כשדים וינצל וילך אל ריעיו אל ההרים ויספר

        להם את כל המוצאות אות‹ו›:   וישובו עמו מן ההרים ששים ושמחים

        בשם יי ואין דובר דבר אליהם ויקראו את שם המקום אלהי אברם:

---

[10]The MS has ויתננהו.

[11]The name Abram seems misplaced in the Hebrew text.

[12]Again it seems necessary to emend MS על to עם. *LAB* has *cum*.

[13]*LAB* has 83500.

[14]Sense and *LAB* (*illi*) demand emending the MS אורם to אותו.

[15]*LAB* has *Et cognominaverunt locum illum nomine Abrae et lingue Chaldeorum Deli, quod interpretatur Deus. Deli* may be *Beli* (Artapanus in *Eusebius' Preparatio Evangelica* 9.18.2). At any rate, *CJ's* version is much simpler.

And the leader said to him: "Your blood be upon your own
head if you do not flee with these men, for if you flee you
will be rescued." And Abram said: "I will not flee but I
will stay."

6.12 And they took Abram and put him[10] in prison. And the leader
sent the eleven men in the care of 50 men to the mountains,
and also he sent food for them with ten camels in the care of
50 others. And he commanded them to remain with them for
fifteen days and to return saying: "We have not found them."
"And if you do not do this, I will burn you in the fire."

6.13 And after seven days all the people gathered and said to
their leaders: "Give us the men who were not willing to be
part of our plan, and let us burn them in the fire." And they
sent to bring them, but there was no one there but Abram.

6.14 And Pinḥas and Nimrod the leaders said to Joktan the leader:
"Where are the men who were imprisoned in the jail at your
house?" And Joktan said to them: "Behold they broke out
tonight and escaped, and I sent 100 men after them to seek
them out and kill them."

6.15 And all the people said: "Behold, we have not found anyone
except Abram; let us burn him in the fire."
And they took Abram and made him stand before the leaders and
questioned him saying: "Where are the men whom we locked up
with you?" And Abram said: "I do not know for I was sleeping
tonight; and when I awoke, I did not find them."

6.16 And they made an oven, a kiln, and they heated it until the
fire along with the brick was kindled. And they put Abram[11]
⟨with⟩[12] the brick in the kiln of fire, and Joktan abated the
wrath of all the people with the burning of Abram.

6.17 And the Lord caused a great earthquake in all the earth, and
the fire went forth from the kiln and became a flame and de-
voured all the men who were around the kiln. And the number
of those burned on that day was 84500.[13] But Abram was not
burned by the fire.

6.18 And he went forth from the kiln, from Ur (= the fire) of the
Chaldees, and he was rescued. And he went to his companions
in the mountains and told them all that happened to ⟨him⟩.[14]
And they returned with him from the mountains, happy and re-
joicing in the name of the Lord. And no one was saying a
word to them. And they called the name of the place "the God
of Abram."[15]

30.1   ריהי אחר הדברים האלה והעם לא שבו ממועדנותיהם הרעים ריבואו אל

נשיאיהם ריאמרו הנה לא ינצח אדם את העולם: הבה ונבנה לנו עיר

ומגדל וראשו בשמים אשר לא יחדל לעולם:

2   ריהי כי החלו לבנות וירא יי את העיר ואת המגדל ריאמר הן עם אחד

ושפה אחת לכולם ועתה הארץ לא תסבול וגם השמים לא תשא להם:

3   לכן הנני מפיצם בכל הארץ ואבל{ב}ל את לשונם אשר לא יכור איש את

אחיר ולא ישמע איש את שפת רעהו ר<א>צום אל הסלעים: יהיו להם

משכנות בקנים ובקש ריחפרו להם מערות ומחילות עפר וחירת השדה ישבו

עמם ריהיו שם כל הימים ולא יזמר עוד לעשות כאלה 'ואקרבם בצינות':

מהם אכלה במים ומהם אכלה באש גם בצמא אשחיתם:

7.4=   ואבחר באברם עבדי ואוציא אותו מארצם ואביאנו אל הארץ (אשר)

עינ<יי>י מקדם בה:

4   ריהי כאשר חטאו לפני ב<נ>י תבל והבאתי המבול עליהם והארץ ההיא

לא נשחתה כי לא ירד עליה מבול בחמתי: ואושיב שם את אברם עבדי

ואכרת לו ולזרעו ברית עד עולם ואברכהו ואהיה לו לאלהים עד עולם:

5   ריהי כאשר החלו לבנות את המגדל ריבל{ב}ל יי את לשונם וישנה

דמותם לדמות קופים ולא הכיר איש את אחיר ולא הבין איש שפת רעהו

---

[1] The phrase וראשו בשמים is not in *LAB*.

[2] Perhaps we should read תשאו rather than תשא.

[3] We should read ואבלל (after Gen 11.9) rather than MS ואבלבל.

[4] The *ḥeth* in אחיר is blurred, but the reading is certain.

[5] *CJ* has singular ישמע while MT has plural ישמעו.

[6] We have read ואצום rather than MS ויצום; cf. *LAB commendabo eos petris*.

[7] יהיר is blurred, but the reading is almost certain. *LAB* has *et edificabunt*.

[8] James's (p. 247) emendation of Latin *scuto* to *sputo* on the basis of Isa 40.15 (LXX) and *LAB* 12.4 (*tamquam sputum estimabitur*) as well as 4 Ezra 6.56 and 2 Bar 82.5 is correct. *CJ* clearly was reading *scuto* in the *LAB* MS and then trying to make sense out of an already corrupt text.

[9] Some connecting word such as אשר or ו is needed. *LAB* has ... *in terram quam respexit*.

[10] The MS has עינרי. *LAB* has *oculus meus*.

[11] We have read בני for MS ביי. *LAB* has *inhabitantes*.

7.1   And after these events the people did not turn from their
         evil schemings, and they came to their leaders and *said:*   "Be-
         hold, will not man conquer the world? *Come, let us build for
         ourselves a city and a tower, (and its top will be in the
         heavens)*[1] (Gen 11.4) which will never come to an end."

7.2   And when they began to build, the Lord saw *the city and the
         tower, and* he *said: "Behold one people, and there is one
         language for all* (Gen 11.5-6). And now the earth will not
         bear them, and also the heavens will not take[2] them.

7.3   Therefore, behold I am scattering them in all the earth, and
         I will confuse[3] their speech so that a man will not under-
         stand his brother[4] and *a man will not* hear[5] *the language of
         his neighbor* (Gen 11.7). And ⟨I⟩ will order[6] them to the
         cliffs. There will be[7] dwellings for them made out of reeds
         and straw, and they will dig for themselves caves and holes
         in the ground, and the beasts of the field will dwell with
         them. And they will be there all the days, and they will not
         plan to do deeds such as these again. And ʾI will draw near
         them with shields (thorns?)ʾ.[8] Part of them I will annihilate
         with water, and part of them I will annihilate with fire.
         Also with thirst I will destroy them.

7.4   And I will choose Abram my servant, and I will bring him out
         of their land and will bring him to the land (on which)[9] ⟨my
         eyes⟩[10] have rested from of old.
         And it happened that, when the ⟨people⟩[11] of the earth sinned
         before me, then I brought the flood upon them. But that land
         was not destroyed, for the flood did not descend upon it in
         my wrath. And I will make Abram my servant dwell there, and
         I will make for him and for his seed an eternal covenant.
         And I will bless him and will be for him for a God forever."

7.5   And when they began to build the tower, the Lord confused[12]
         their speech and changed their form to the form of monkeys.[13]
         And a man did not understand his brother, *and a man did not*
         comprehend *the language of his neighbor.* And when the builders
         gave a command to bring the stones they brought the water;
         and when they said to bring the water, they brought the straw.

_____

[12]Again the MS has the בלל form (יבלבל); see note 3 to this
chapter.
[13]The equivalent of "to the form of monkeys" is not in *LAB*.

ויהי כאשר צירו הבנאים להביא את האבנים ויביאו את המים וכאשר

אמרו להביא את המים הביאו את הקש: על כן הופר(ו) מזימותם ויחדלו

לבנות את המגדל ויפץ יי אותם משם על פני כל הארץ:

[*CJ* 30.6-42.4 presents another version of the tower story (30.6-8),
more genealogies (31), Nimrod's dynasty (32), Nimrod and Abraham
(33), Abraham's destruction of the idols (34), Abraham's further exploits and the birth of Jacob (35), the military victories of Jacob's
sons (36), the battle between the sons of Judah and Esau (37), the
testament of Naphtali (38), Joseph and Potiphar's wife (39), the
sons of Noah according to the *Josippon* (40), the kings of Rome (41)
and Israel's fate in Egypt (42.1-4).

In this way their evil designs were frustrated[14] *and they
ceased building* the tower.[15] *And the Lord scattered them
from there over the face of all the earth* (Gen 11.7-8).

[*LAB* 8.1-9.1 tells how Abraham dwelt in Canaan and became the father
of Isaac, and presents lists of Isaac's and Esau's wives, Isaac's
sons, Jacob's wives and sons. The revenge by Jacob's sons on
Shechem, the descent into Egypt, the genealogies of the twelve patri-
archs, and the persecution in Egypt are also recounted.]

---

[14]We have emended singular הופר to plural הופרו.

[15]MT has עיר, and *LAB* has *civitatem* in Gen 11.8 while LXX and
Samaritan Pentateuch have "city" and "tower." *CJ* has only "tower."

42.5 ויאספו הזקנים וכל העם ויבכו ויספדו: לוּ יְשֻׁכְּלוּ רַחֲמֵי נשותינו כי
פרי בטנינו לאין: ועתה נתן זמן שלא יקרב איש אל אשתו כי טוב לנו
למות בלא בנים מראת את בנותינו טמאות ביד ערלים עד אשר נדע מה
יעשה יי:

9.3= ויען עמרם ויאמר הטוב בעיניכם אשר במצוק ימעט העולם או באין משפם
יכרת העולם: אם לב התחומות יגיש עד שחק ‹לא›זרע ישראל יכלה:
ויי נשבע לאברהם לענות את זרעו ארבע מאות שנה והנה עברו מברית
בין הבתרים אשר כרת את אברהם שלש מאות וחמשים שנה ואשר נשתעבדנו
במצרים מאת ושלשים שנה:

9.4= ועתה לא אעמוד בעצמכם לתת זמן במעשה יי למנוע את אשתי למלא את
הארץ כי לא לנצח יחרה אף יי ולא לעולמים יזנח עמו ולא על און כרת
ברית עם אבותינו ולא לריק הרבה את זרע ישראל:

6   ועתה אלכה אל אשתי כמצות יי ואם טוב בעיניכם עשׂו כמוני והיה כאשר
תהר נשותינו תצפנו את בטן הריתם עד שלשה חדשים כאשר עשתה תמר
אמינו אשר אין במזימתה לזנות מאחרי ישראל כי אמרה טוב לי למות
מלערב עם הגוים: ותצפן את בטנה עד שלשה חדשים ותתודה:

9.6= ועתה נעשה כן גם אנחנו וכאשר ימלאו עת לדתנה ולא נמנע את פרי
בטנינו ומי יודע אם בזה יקנא יי וירשיענו מעינייננו:

7   וייטב בעיני יי את דברי עמרם ויאמר יי דבר(י) ך יטיבו בעיני:
לכן ילוד לך בן עבד לי לעולם לעשות פלאות בבית יעקב ואותות
ומופתים בעמים וראאה לו את כבודי ואודיעהו את דרכיי:

---

[1]The sentence is not in *LAB*.

[2]או is the MS reading, but לא or אז or even אך would make better sense. Perhaps, "Shall the heart..., or will the seed...."

[3]The MS has דברך יטיבו; either the noun should be made plural
(as we have done) or the verb made singular (as we could just as
easily have done). Our choice is governed by the preceding sentence.

9.2   And the elders and all the people gathered together and wept
        and lamented: "Would that the wombs of our wives were barren,
        for the fruit of our wombs is to be annihilated! And now set
        a time when a man will not approach his wife, for it is bet-
        ter for us to die without sons than to see our daughters de-
        filed by Gentiles until we know what the Lord will do."

9.3   And Amram answered and said: "Is it better in your eyes that
        the world be diminished by constraint or that the world
        be cut away unjustly?[1]   If the heart of the deeps should
        reach the heaven, the seed of Israel will ⟨not⟩[2] perish.
        And the Lord swore to Abraham to afflict his seed for four
        hundred years (see Gen 15.13), and there have passed from the
        covenant between the pieces which he made with Abraham three
        hundred and fifty years, and of these we have been enslaved
        in Egypt one hundred and thirty years.

9.4   And now I will not stand for your plan to set a time for the
        work of the Lord, to hold back my wife from filling the
        earth, for not forever will the anger of the Lord be kindled
        and not unto eternity will he reject his people and not out
        of perversity has he made a covenant with our fathers and not
        in vain has he multiplied the seed of Israel.

9.5   And now I will go to my wife according to the commandment of
        the Lord; and if it is good in your eyes, do as I do. And
        when our wives conceive, you will conceal the womb of their
        conception for three months as Tamar our mother did (see Gen
        38.24-25).
        This was not by design to turn from Israel, for she said:
        'It is better for me to die than to mingle with the heathen.'
        And she concealed her womb for three months, and she made a
        confession.

9.6   And now let us also act in this way. And when the time of
        bearing is fulfilled and we do not hold back the fruit of our
        wombs, who knows if over this the Lord will become zealous
        and save us from our afflictions?"

9.7   And the words of Amram were pleasing in the eyes of the Lord,
        and the Lord said: "Your word(s)[3] are pleasing in my eyes.
        Therefore there will be born to you a son, my servant forever,
        to do marvels in the house of Jacob and signs and wonders
        among the nations. And I will show him my glory and will
        make him know my ways.

9.8=   ואדליק נרי בו ואלמדהו את עדותיי ותורותיי ואדריכהו על במותי

צדקותיי ומשפטיי ואור עולם תאיר לו: כי עליו חשבתי מקדם לאמר לא

ידון רוחי באדם לעלם בשגם הוא בשר והיו ימיו מאה ועשרים שנה:

8   וילך עמרם משבט לוי ויקח את יוכבד בת לוי אשתו ויקחו כל העם את

נשיהם ויהי לעמרם בן ובת אחרון ומרים:

9.10=   ותחל רוח יי במרים והיא בחלום הלילה ותגד לאביה לאמר ראיתי הלילה

והנה איש לבוש שני: אמר לי אמרי לאביך ולאמך הנה אשר נולד מכם

הלילה יושלך ויובא במים ועל ידו יבשה המים: ואותות ומופתים יעשו

בו ויושיע את עמי ישראל ויהיה מוהלם לעלם: ותגד מרים את החלום

לאביה ולאמה ולא האמינו לה:

9   ותהר יוכבד ששה חדשים ויהי בחדש השביעי ותלד בן: ולא יכלה עוד

הצפינו כי בתים עשה להם לידע את לדת   '20 ±'ׁ:

9.14=   ויאמרו הזקנים אל עמרם הלא זה דברינו אשר דברנו אליך כי טוב לנו

למות בלא בנים מראות פרי בטנינו מושלך במים ויאמר עמרם אל מרים

בתו איה נבואת חלומיך: ותתיצב אחותו מרחוק לידע מה יעשה לו:

9.15=   ותרד בת פרעה לרחוץ ותקח את הילד ויהי לה לבן:

[CJ 43.1-56.4 has the *Chronicle of Moses* (43-48) which tells of
Moses' birth (43), his concealment and discovery, his flight from
Egypt (44), his stay in Cush (45), Pharaoh's plan to destroy Israel
(46), Moses' appearance before the royal court (47), and the plagues
and the subsequent exodus (48). There are also accounts of Aaron's
death (49), Moses' death (50), Moses' special merit and other matters

---

[4] *LAB* has *superexcellentiam meam et iusticias et iudicia.*

[5] Gaster (p. 105) translates: "and through him shall the light
of the world be kindled." *LAB* has *et lumen sempiternum luceam ei.*

[6] *LAB* has *in veste bissina*; scarlet = שני and byssus = שש.

[7] The reading מוהלם is orthographically certain. Gaster (p.
106) translates as "their leader." *LAB* has *et ipse ducatum eius
aget semper.*

[8] The sense of the first part ("made houses") is difficult, and
the reading of the second part is impossible. *LAB* has *quia rex
Egipti preposuerat principes locorum, ut quando parerent Hebree
statim in flumen proicerent masculos eorum.* Gaster (p. 106) avoids
the problem: "for the Egyptians had made houses by which they knew
of the birth of a child. They therefore made a little ark and
placed the child among the bulrushes." There are not enough spaces
for all that is in Gaster's version. Perhaps, read בתים (ראשי) in
the first part (M. Stone).

9.8   And I will light my lamp in him and teach him my statutes and
       my laws. And I will lead him over the heights of my righteous-
       ness and judgments.[4] And the eternal light will shine forth
       for him.[5] For of him I have thought from of old saying: '*My
       spirit will not abide in man forever, for he is flesh; and
       his days will be one hundred and twenty years'* (Gen 6.3)."

9.9   *And Amram* from the tribe *of Levi went and took Jochebed the
       daughter of Levi* (Exod 2.1; 6.20) as his wife, and all the
       people took their wives. And Amram had a son and a daughter,
       Aaron and Miriam.

9.10   And the spirit of the Lord disturbed Miriam, and she was in a
       dream by night. And she told her father, saying: "I have
       seen tonight, and behold, a man dressed in scarlet.[6] He said
       to me: 'Say to your father and your mother: "Behold that
       which is born from you tonight will be cast forth and put in
       the waters, and by him the waters will be dried up. And
       signs and wonders will be done by him, and he will save my
       people Israel. And he will be their circumciser[7] forever."'"
       And Miriam told the dream to her father and mother, and they
       did not believe her.

[*LAB* 9.11 summarizes the sufferings of Israel.]

9.12   *And* Jochebed *was pregnant* for six months, and it happened in
       the seventh month that *she bore a son. And she was no longer
       able to conceal him* (Exod 2.2-3) for he made houses for them
       to know the birth [± 20].[8]

[*LAB* 9.13 says that Moses was born circumcised.]

9.14   And the elders said to Amram: "Are not these our words which
       we spoke to you, that it is better for us to die without sons
       than to see the fruit of our wombs cast forth on the waters?"
       And Amram said to Miriam his daughter: "Where is the prophecy
       of your dreams?" *And his sister stationed herself from afar
       to know what would be done to him* (Exod 2.4).

9.15   *And the daughter of Pharaoh went down to bathe* (Exod 2.5). *And
 -16   she took the child, and he was as a son to her* (Exod 2.9-10).

[*LAB* 10.1-24.6 deals with the crossing of the Red Sea (10), the giv-
ing of the Law (11), the golden calf (12), rules for furnishing the
altar, the sacrifices and festivals (13), the census of the people
(14), the spies (15), the rebellion of Korah (16), the choice of the
priestly family (17), the deeds of Balaam (18), the death of Moses

concerning him (51), his reception into heaven (52), Israel's order
in the wilderness (53), the smiting of the firstborn (54), the rebellion of Korah (55), and history from Joshua to the Judges (56).]

(19), Joshua as Moses' successor (20), the building of the altar
(21), the schismatical altar (22), the farewell speech of Joshua
(23) and the death of Joshua (24).]

57.1 ויאמר פֿילו ריע יוסף בן גוריון בספרו כי כאשר מת יהושע לא היה
      לישראל רועה להנהיגם וישאלו בני ישראל ביי מי יעלה לפניהם להלחם
      בכנעני בתחילה: ויאמר יי אם לב העם הזה שלם עם יי יהודה יעלה
      ואם לא יעלה: ויוסף לשאל במה נדע את לב העם: ויאמר יי הקרבת
      בגורלות לשבטיכם והיה השבט אשר ילכדנו יי יקרב למשפחות ותדעו את
      לב העם:

2   ריען העם ויאמרו אל יי הפקד עלינו ראש וקצין להקריבנו בגורלות
      ואשר יוציאנו ואשר יביאנו: ויען מלאך יי לאמר שלחו גורל בשבט כלב
      והיה הנלכד בגורל הוא יהיה לכם לראש ולקצין: ויעשו כן וַיֵּצֵא
      הגורל על קנז ויעמידוהו לשר על ישראל:

=25.3 ויאמר קנז אל העם הביאו אלי את שבטיכם ושמעו בקול יי ויבאו אליו:
3   ויאמר אליהם אתם ידעתם כי משה עבד יי צוה לכם לאמר לא תסורו מן
      הדרך אשר צויתי לכם בתורה ימין ושמאול וגם יהושע הזהיר אתכם כן:
4   ועתה הנה שמענו מיי כל כי לב העם הזה אין אתו וציונו אשר נקרב
      בגורל לשבטינו ואל יחרה אף יי בנו ואם אני וביתי נלכד תשרפונו
      באש ויאמרו בו העם טוב הדבר:

5   ויקרבו השבטים בגורל לפניו וילכדו משבט יהודה שלש מאות וארבעים
      וחמשה איש ומשבט ראובן חמש מאות וארבעים ומשבט שמעון שלש מאות
      ושלשים וחמשה ומשבט לוי שלש מאות וחמשים ומשבט יששכר שש מאות
      ושים וחמשה ומשבט זבולון חמש מאות וארבעים וחמשה . . . . ומשבט
      גד שלש מאות ושמונים ומשבט אשר שש מאות ושים וחמשה ומשבט מנשה
      ארבע מאות ושמונים ומשבט אפרים ארבע מאות ושים ושמונה . . . . .
6   ויהי מספר הנלכדים ששת אלפים ומאה ועשר ויתנם קנז במשמר לשאול
      להם על פי יי:

---

[1]The compiler of *CJ* apparently identifies the author of these
texts with Philo Judaeus.

[2]Presumably, there was no need to repeat לֹא.

[3]*LAB* has 560 for Reuben.

[4]*LAB* has 150 for Levi - a disproportionately low figure.

[5]As in *LAB*, the tribes of Dan and Naphthali have been omitted.

[6]*LAB* adds *et de tribu Beniamin*, CCLXVII.

25.1   And Philo,[1] the friend of Joseph son of Gurion, said in his
       book that when Joshua died there was no shepherd for Israel,
       to lead them. *And the sons of Israel asked the Lord who
       would go up* before them *to fight first against the Canaanite*
       (Jdgs 1.1). And the Lord said: "If the heart of this people
       is perfect with the Lord, Judah will go up; if not, no one[2]
       will go up." And they continued to ask: "How will we know
       the heart of the people?" And the Lord said: "Arrange your
       tribes in lots, and the tribe which the Lord will choose will
       be arranged according to families; and you will know the heart
       of the people."

25.2   And the people answered and said to the Lord: "Appoint over
       us a chief and a ruler to arrange us in lots, and one who
       will bring us out and who will bring us in." And the angel
       of the Lord answered, saying: "Cast a lot in the tribe of
       Caleb, and he who is chosen in that lot will be for you a
       chief and a ruler." And they did so, and the lot fell to
       Kenaz, and they appointed him prince over Israel.

25.3   And Kenaz said to the people: "Bring to me your tribes and
       hear the voice of the Lord." And they came to him.
       And he said to them: "You know that Moses the servant of the
       Lord commanded you, saying: 'You shall not turn from the way
       which I commanded you in the Law to the right or left (see
       Deut 28.14; Jos 1.7).' And also Joshua warned you in this way.
       And now behold we all have heard from the Lord that the
       heart of this people is not with him, and he has commanded us
       that we should be arranged by lot according to our tribes;
       and let not the anger of the Lord be kindled against us. And
       if I and my house be chosen you will burn us in the fire."
       And the people said about this: "This word is good."

25.4   And the tribes were arranged by lot before him; and they were
       chosen from the tribe of Judah 345 men, and from the tribe of
       Reuben 540,[3] and from the tribe of Simeon 335, and from the
       tribe of Levi 350,[4] and from the tribe of Issachar 665, and
       from the tribe of Zebulun 545,[5] . . . . and from the tribe of
       Gad 380, and from the tribe of Asher 665, and from the tribe
       of Manasseh 480, and from the tribe of Ephraim 468[6] . . . .
       And the number of those chosen were 6110. And Kenaz put them
       in custody to ask about the word of the Lord for them.

25.5= ויאמר קנז על אלה אמר משה עבד יי פן יש בכם שרש פורה ראש ולענה וברוך יי אשר גילה לנו את החטאים אשר לא נכשל בהם:

7   ויתפלל קנז ואלעזר הכהן וכל זקני העדה אל יי לאמר אתה יי הודעת את האנשים אשר לא האמינו בנפלאותיך אשר עשית את אבותינו בהוציאם מארץ מצרים עד היום הזה:

8   ויאמר יי שאל נא את פיהם והתודו את ערנם ותשרפו אותם באש:

25.7= ויאמר להם קנז אתם ידעתם כי עכן בן זבדי מעל בחרם ונלכד בגורל והתודה את חטאתו: גם אתם תנו תודה ליי ותחיו עם אשר יחיה יי בתחיית המתים:

9   ויען אחד מהם ושמו אֵלָה ולא נמות כי אם באש ועתה שאל את פי כל שבט לבד:

25.9= וישאל קנז את פי יהודה שבטו ויאמרו הנה בחרנו לעשות לנו את העגל כאשר עשר את אבותינו במדבר:

10   וישאל לשבט ראובן ויאמרו לזבוח בחרנו לאלהי העמים: ובני לוי אמרו בחרנו לבחון ולנסות אם המשכן קודש הוא: ובני יששכר אמרו בחרנו לשאול באלילים מה יהיה לנו:

11   ויאמרו בני זבולון בחר(נו) לאכול בשר בנינו ובנותינו למען נדע אם חפץ בהם יי: ויאמרו בני דן בחרנו ללמ<ו>ד לבנינו את אשר למדנו מן האמורי הנה הספרים גנוזים וטמונים תחת הר העברים ושם תמצאם וישלח קנז וימצאם:

12   וישאל לבני נפתלי ויאמרו עשינו ככל מעשה האמורי אשר עשר והטמינום באהל אֵלָה אשר אמר לך לשאל לכל שבט ושבט לבד וישלח קנז וימצאם שם:

---

[7] Our translation has been guided by *LAB Numquid non iam aderit nobis mors ut moriamur in igne?*

[8] As in *LAB*, the tribe of Simeon has been omitted.

[9] The MS has only בחר rather than בחרנו.

[10] The MS has ללמוד ("to learn"). *LAB* has *ut doceremus filios nostros.*

[11] *LAB* has *sub monte Abrahae* which could conceivably refer to Mount Moriah.

25.5   And Kenaz said: "Concerning these Moses the servant of the
        Lord said: '*Lest there be among you a root bearing poisonous
        and bitter fruit*' (Deut 29.17) and blessed is the Lord who
        has revealed to us the sinners so that we would not stumble
        on account of them."

25.6   And Kenaz and Eleazar the priest and all the elders of the
        congregation prayed to the Lord saying: "You, Lord, have
        made known the men who did not believe your wonders which you
        have done with our fathers in leading them out from the land
        of Egypt until this day."
        And the Lord said: "Ask them, I pray.   And they will confess
        their sin; and you will burn them in the fire."

25.7   And Kenaz said to them: "You know that Achan the son of
        Zabdi acted treacherously in the matter of the ban, and he
        was chosen by lot and confessed his sin.   You also make a con-
        fession to the Lord, and you will live along with whomever
        the Lord will revive in the resurrection of the dead."

25.8   And one of them answered, and his name was Elah: "Will we
        not die in the fire?[7]   And now ask every tribe individually."

25.9   And Kenaz asked Judah his own tribe, and they said: "Behold
        we chose to make for ourselves the calf as they did with our
        fathers in the wilderness."
        And he asked the tribe of Reuben, and they said: "We chose
        to sacrifice to the gods of the nations."[8]   And the sons of
        Levi said: "We chose to try and to test whether the taber-
        nacle is holy."   And the sons of Issachar said: "We chose to
        ask the idols what will happen to us."
        And the sons of Zebulun said: "We chose[9] to eat the flesh of
        our sons and our daughters in order to know if the Lord loves
        them."   And the sons of Dan said: "We chose to teach[10] our
        sons what we learned from the Amorite.   Behold the books are
        hidden and concealed beneath Mount Abarim,[11] and there you
        will find them."   And Kenaz sent and found them.
        And he asked the sons of Naphthali, and they said: "We made
        everything the Amorites made, and we have concealed them in
        the tent of Elah who told you to ask each and every tribe
        individually."   And Kenaz sent and found them there.

13   ויאמרו בני גד אנחנו שכבנו את נשי עמיתינו: גם בני אשר אמרו
אנחנו מצאנו שבעה עצבי זהב אשר קראום האמורי קדשי נִנְפֵי ועמם
אבנים יקרות אשר עליהם והטמינום תחת הר שכם שלח נא שמה ותמצאם
וישלח וימצא אותם:

25.11=   והמה העצבים אשר הגידו לאמורי כל מעשיהם לעתים:

14   ואלה שמות שבעה אנשים החטאים אשר עשר אותם אחר המבול כנען פוט
שלח נמרוד אֶלָה דיעול שוח: ולא היה כתבניתם מעשה ידי חרש עוד

25.12=   והאבנים מארץ חוילה אשר שם הבדולה ואבן השהם: ואלה האבנים יקרות
היו לאמורי לעצבים ולא 'תסולם' דבר כי בלילה היו מאירים כאור
יומם וגם כאשר האמורי העיוורים היו מנקשים את העצבים ונוגעים את
האבנים בעיניהם היו רואים: ויקחם קנז וישמרם עד יוודע מה יעשה מהם:

15   וישאל עוד קנז לבני מנשה ויאמרו לא שמרנו את השבת לקדשו: ורבני
אפרים אמרו רצונינו להעביר בנינו ובנותינו באש כמשפט האמורי:
ורבני בנימין אמרו חפצנו לבחון את ספר התורה אם מיי היא אם מאת
משה היא:

26.1=   ויכתב קנז את דבריהם בספר ויקראם לפני יי:

16   ויאמר אליו יי קח את האנשים האלה ואת כל אשר תמצא אתם ואת כל אשר
להם והורדתם אל נ<ח>ל פישרון ושם תשרפם באש:

26.2=   ויאמר קנז גם את האבנים יקרות אשר אין ערכם נשרפם או נקדישם אליך
ויאמר   יי אם אלהים יקח מן החרם אף כי בני האדם:

---

[12] See *LAB que vocabant Amorrei sanctas nimphas.*

[13] *LAB* has these last two names as one *Desuath*, but this may be
a corruption of *Dedan Suah* (cf. Gen 10.7), or perhaps it is רשעתים
of Jdgs 3.8 read as דשעתים.

[14] *LAB* has *quorum precium ideo inestimabile erat.*

[15] For "everything" we follow *LAB*'s *ea que inventa sunt.*

[16] The MS has נהל.

25.10   And the sons of Gad said: "We have slept with the wives of our neighbors." Also the sons of Asher said: "We found seven golden idols which the Amorites called the 'holy to the nymphs'[12] and along with them precious stones which were upon them, and we concealed them beneath Mount Shechem. Send there, we pray, and you will find them." And he sent, and he found them.

25.11   And they were the idols which told the Amorites all their deeds at particular times.

And these are the names of the seven sinful men who made them after the flood: Canaan, Puṭ, Šelaḥ, Nimrod, 'Elah, Dî'ûl, Šûah.[13] And the work of a skilled craftsman is not executed according to their pattern any more. And the stones were from *the land of Havilah where there are bdellium and onyx stone* (Gen 2.11-12).

25.12   And these precious stones were idols for the Amorite, and their ⸢ ? ⸣ was priceless,[14] for by night they were shining like the light of day; and also when the blind Amorites were kissing the idols and touching the stones with their eyes, they could see. And Kenaz took them and guarded them until it would be known what would become of them.

25.13   And Kenaz again asked the sons of Manasseh, and they said: "We have not observed the sabbath to sanctify it." And the sons of Ephraim said: "It was our good pleasure to make our sons and our daughters pass through the fire according to the Amorite custom." And the sons of Benjamin said: "We desired to try the book of the Law whether it is from the Lord or is from Moses."

26.1   And Kenaz wrote their words in a book and read them before the Lord.

And the Lord said to him: "Take these men and everything[15] which you find with them and everything which is theirs; and bring them down to the river[16] Pishon, and there you will burn them in the fire."

26.2   And Kenaz said: "Shall we also burn the precious stones which are invaluable, or shall we dedicate them to you?" And the Lord said: "If God will take from the ban, how much more the sons of man!

17   קח נא את הספרים ואת האבנים הטובים לשמור עד אשר אודיעך מה תעשה
מהם ובמה תאבדם כי אש לא תאכלם ואת האנשים תשרף באש ויאמרו כל
העם ככה יעשה לאיש אשר יסור את לבבו מיי:

18   והיה כאשר תשרפם קח את האבנים הטובות אשר לא תשרפם אש ואשר הברזל
לא יוכל להם ותנם בראש ההר אצל מזבח החדש ושם אצוה על העבים
להוריד עליהם את טלם למחותם:

=26.4   ואצוה למלאכי ליקח את האבנים הטובות להשליכם בעמוקי הים אשר לא
יראו עוד ולהעלות לי תחתיהם שנים עשר אבנים טובות מאלה ונתת
אותם אל האפוד ואל החשן וקדש אותם לי:

19   וילך קנז ויקח את כל הנמצא עם האנשים החטאים וידבר אל העם לאמר
אתם ראיתם נוראות ונפלאות אשר הראנו יי עד היום הזה ואשר הודיענו
את האנשים החטאים להשיב להם כעלילותם:

20   ועתה ארור האיש אשר יעשה כן בישראל: ויענו כל העם אמן וישרפום
באש:

=26.6   ואחר לקח קנז את האבנים ורצה לבחון אותם באש ויכבה האש ויקח לו
ברזל לכתותם ויפץ הברזל מפניהם:

21   וגם את ספריהם נתן במים למחותם ויבש המים מעליהם ויאמר קנז ברוך
יי היום אשר עשה נפלאות ונוראות עם בני אדם כאשר יחטאו ולא יכחשר:

=26.7   ויקח את האבנים ואת הספרים ויתנם בהר כאשר צוהו יי אצל מזבח החדש
ויעל עליו זבחים שלמים ויאכלו שם כל העם יחדיו:

22   ויהי בלילה ההיא ויעש יי לאבנים ולספרים כאשר דבר:

=26.9   ויהי בבקר וימצא קנז את שנים עשר אבנים הטובות מפותחות פיתוחי
חותם את שמות בני ישראל:

Take, I pray, the books and the fine stones to guard until I
let you know what you should do with them and how you will
destroy them, for fire will not consume them. But the men
you will burn in the fire. And all the people will say:
'Thus shall it be done to a man who will turn away his heart
from the Lord.'

26.3   And it will happen that when you burn them, take the fine
stones which fire will not burn and which the iron will not
conquer, and put them on the top of the mountain beside the
new altar. And there I will command the clouds to bring down
upon them their dew to destroy them.

26.4   And I will command my angel to take the fine stones, to cast
them into the depths of the sea so that they will not be seen
again, and to bring up for me in their place twelve stones
better than these. And you will place them on the ephod and
on the breastplate, and sanctify them to me."

26.5   And Kenaz came and took everything which was found with the
sinful men, and he spoke to the people saying: "You have
seen the awesome and wonderful things which the Lord has
shown us until this day and which have made known to us the
sinful men so as to requite them according to their evil
deeds.
And now cursed is the man who will act in this way in Israel."
And all the people answered: "Amen." And they burned them
in the fire.

26.6   And afterwards Kenaz took the stones and wished to try them
in the fire, and the fire was extinguished. And he took for
himself iron to crush them, and the iron was broken apart by
them.
And also their books he put in the water to blot them out,
and the water dried up before them. And Kenaz said: "Blessed
is the Lord this day who has done wonderful and awesome things
with the sons of man, for they sin but do not deceive (him)."

26.7   And he took the stones and the books, and he put them on the
mountain as the Lord commanded him beside the new altar. And
he offered upon it sacrifices (peace offerings), and all the
people ate there together.

26.8   And in that night the Lord did with the stones and the books
as he said.

26.9   And in the morning Kenaz found the twelve fine stones *engraved
like the engravings of a signet* (Exod 39.6) with the names of
the sons of Israel.

=26.12　ויאמר יי קח את האבנים האלה ושמתם בארון עם לוחות עד אשר יבנה

שלמה בית לשמי ויתנם על שני הכרובים והיו לי לזכרון על בני ישראל:

23　　והיה כמלאות חטאת בני האדם　לחלל את הבית אשר עשו לי ואקח את

האבנים האלה ואת הלוחות ואתנם במקום אשר נלקחו שם מקדם ויהיו שם

עד קץ זכרון עולם בפוקדי יושבי הארץ ואקחם ויהיו לאור עולם

לאוהבי ולשומרי מצותי וחפרה הלבנה ובושה החמה מפני אורם כי

שבעתיים יאירו מהם:

24　　ויקם קנז ויאמר הנה טובות רבות אשר עשה אלהים ונלקחו בחטאות האדם

ועתה ידעתי כי מעשה האדם תוהו וחייהם הבל:

25　　ויקח קנז את האבנים ממקומם אשר ניתנו ויאירו בכל הארץ כאור השמש

בצהרים וישם אותם אל ארון העדות עם לוחות הברית כאשר צוהו יי

ויהיו שם עד היום הזה:

26　　ויבחר קנז שלש מאות אלף איש חלוצי צבא ביום חשיני למלחמה ויהרגו

חמשת אלפים באויביהם:

=27.2　ויהי ביום השלישי וידבר העם בקנז לאמר הנה קנז עם נשיר ועם

פילגשיו בביתו ואנחנו נחלץ למלחמה על איבינו להשמידם:

27　　וישמעו עבדי קנז ויגידו לו ויאמר להביא את שרי החמשים אליו ויצום

לתח את שלשים ושבעה האנשים אשר דברו עליו רעה אל בית הסהר ויעשו

כן:

28　　ויאמר כאשר יעשה יי תשועה לעמו אמית את האנשים האלה:

=27.5　ויצו אל שר החמשיו לאמר לכה בחרת לי מעבדיי שלש מאות איש בשלש

מאות סוסים ואל יוודע צאחינו למלחמה ויהיו נכונים לצאת עמי הלילה:

---

[17] *LAB* has *Iahel*.　Louis Ginzberg in *The Legends of the Jews* (volume VI, p. 183) notes that אחיאל is one of Solomon's 10 names. *CJ* avoids this matter by simply identifying the temple-builder as Solomon.

[18] האדם is marginal; *LAB* has *peccata populi mei*

[19] *LAB* has *quousque memor sim seculi*.

[20] *LAB* supplies the names of Kenaz's detractors.

[21] The incident described in these paragraphs is loosely based on Jdgs 7.8-18.

[*LAB* 26.10-11 describes the twelve stones.]

26.12   And the Lord said: "Take these stones, and you will place
        them in the ark along with the tablets until Solomon[17] will
        build a temple to my name. And he will place them on the two
        cherubim, and they will be for me a memorial for the sake of
        the sons of Israel.

26.13   And when the sin of the sons of man [18] is complete so as to
        defile the temple which they made for me, then I will take
        these stones and the tablets and will put them in the place
        from where they were taken of old. And they shall be there
        until the time for remembering the world[19]   when I visit
        the inhabitants of the earth. And I will take them, and
        they shall be for an everlasting light for those who love me
        and keep my commandments. And the moon will be confounded
        and the sun ashamed before their light, for they will shine
        seven times more than they do."

26.14   And Kenaz arose and said: "Behold the many good things which
        God has done, but by the sins of man they have been taken
        away. And now I know that the work of man is empty and their
        lives are vanity."

26.15   And Kenaz took the stones from their place where they were
        put, and they shone through all the earth like the light of
        the sun at noon. And he placed them in the ark of the testi-
        mony along with the tablets of the covenant as the Lord com-
        manded him. And they are there until this day.

27.1   And Kenaz chose 300000 men equipped for warfare on the second
        day of the war, and they slew 5000 among their enemies.

27.2   And it happened on the third day that the people spoke against
        Kenaz saying: "Behold Kenaz is with his wives and his concu-
        bines in his house, and we are armed for war against our
        enemies to annihilate them."

27.3   And the servants of Kenaz heard and told it to him. And he
        said to bring the captains of the fifties to him and com-
        manded them to put the thirty-seven men who spoke evil against
        him in the jail. And they did so.

27.4   And he said: "When the Lord works victory for his people, I
        will kill these men."[20]

27.5   And he commanded the captain of his fifties saying: "Go, and
        choose for me   from my servants 300 men with 300 horses.
        And let not our going out for war be known, and let them be
        prepared to go out with me tonight."[21]

29   וישלח קנז מרגלים לראת את מקום חניית האמורי וילכו ויראו כי רבים
הם מאד להלחם על ישראל וישובו ויגידו אל קנז:

30   ויקם קנז הוא ושלש מאות איש אשר אתו לילה ויקח שופר בידו ויהי
כאשר קרב במחנה ויאמר אל עבדיו שבו לכם פה ואלכה לבדי ואראה
במחנה האמורי והיה אם תשמעו את קול השופר תבאו אלי ואם אין תשבו:

31   וירד קנז לבדו ויתפלל ויאמר יי אלהי אבותינו אתה הראית לעבדיך את
כל הגדולות אשר עשית ועתה הפלא נפלאותיך עם עבדך ואלחם באיביך
וידעו כל הגוים כי לא קצרה ידך להושיע ברב או במעט כי אתה יי איש
מלחמה:

32   ויאמר קנז לפני יי זאת אות התשועה אשר תעשה עמי היום והיה כאשר
אריק חרבי מתערתו ואבריק במחנה האמורי אם באלה ידעו האמורי כי
אני קנז ידעתי כי תתנם בידי ואם אין לא שמעת לי כי אם נתתני בידם
בחטאתי:

33   ויהי אחרי זאת וישמע קנז את דברי האמורי לאמר נקומה ונלחמה
בישראל כי אלהינו קדושים נִינְפֵּי בידם והוא יתנם בידינו:

27.9=   ורוח לבשה את קנז ויקם ויבריק את חרבו על האמורי ויראו האמורי
ויאמרו הנה חרב קנז למלאת קבורות ופצעים וידענו כי האלהים אשר
לנו בידם נתנו אתם בידינו ועתה קומו למלחמה עליהם:

34   וישמע קנז את דבריהם וירד אל מחנה האמורי ויך בהם וישלח יי את
גבריאל המלאך ויך את האמורי בסנוירים ויכו אחד את אחד ויכם קנז
ארבעים וחמשה אלף איש לבד: מאשר הכה איש את רעיהו ארבעים וחמשה
אלף:

35   ויהי כאשר הכם קנז וידבק חרבו בכפו והנה איש אמורי נס מן המחנה
ויאמר קנז אליו הן ידעת את אשר עשיתי לאמורי ועתה הגד נא לי במה
אפריד ידי מחרבי ויאמר האמורי הך נא איש עברי ושפוך דמו חם על
ידך ותפרידנו ויך קנז את האיש האמורי ויתן דמו בידו ויפרד:

_____

[22]LAB has *sancte nostre nimphe*.
[23]LAB has *multiplicavit vulneratos nostros*.
[24]In LAB the angel's name is *Ingethel*.

27.6   And Kenaz sent spies to look at the place of the Amorite
        camp, and they went and saw that there were very many to
        fight against Israel. And they returned and told Kenaz.
        And Kenaz and his 300 men who were with him arose that night,
        and he took a ram's horn in his hand. And when he drew near
        to the camp, he said to his servants: "Stay by yourselves
        here, and I will go alone and look at the Amorite camp. And
        if you hear the sound of the ram's horn, you will come to me;
        if not, return home."

27.7   And Kenaz went down alone and prayed and said: "Lord God of
        our fathers, you have shown your servants all the good things
        which you have done. And now work your wonders with your
        servant, and I will fight against your enemies, and all the
        Gentiles will know that your hand is not too short to save
        by many or by few, for you, *Lord, are a man of war* (Exod 15.3)."
        And Kenaz said before the Lord: "This is the sign of the
        victory which you will work with me today: And when I draw
        my sword from its sheath and flash it in the Amorite camp, if
        by these the Amorites know that I am Kenaz, I know that you
        will give them into my hand; and if not, you have not heard
        me but you gave me into their hand on account of my sin."

27.8   And after this Kenaz heard the words of the Amorites saying:
        "Let us arise and fight against Israel, for our gods, the
        holy nymphs,[22] are in their hand and will give them into our
        hands."

27.9   And the spirit clothed Kenaz, and he arose and flashed his
        sword against the Amorites; and the Amorites saw and said:
        "Behold the sword of Kenaz to fill graves and us with
        bruises,[23] and we know that our gods in their hand have given
        them into our hands. And now arise for war against them."

27.10   And Kenaz heard their words and went down to the Amorite camp
        and smote them. And the Lord sent the angel Gabriel,[24] and
        he smote the Amorites with sudden blindness. And they smote
        one another, and Kenaz alone smote 45000 men. Of those who
        smote each man his neighbor 45000.

27.11   And when Kenaz smote them, his sword clung in his palm. And
        behold an Amorite man fled from the camp, and Kenaz said to
        him: "Behold, you know what I have done to the Amorites. And
        now tell me, I pray, how I may separate my hand from my sword."
        And the Amorite said: "Smite, I pray, a Hebrew man and pour
        his hot blood over your hand, and you will separate it." And
        Kenaz smote the Amorite man and put his blood on his hand and
        separated it.

27.12= רישב קנז אל חילו וימצאם ישֵׁנים כי תרדמה נפלה עליהם ולא ידעו את
אשר עשה קנז בלילה ויעורו משנתם ויראו כל השדה מלֵאָה חללים ויתמהו
מאד ויאמר קנז הדרכי יי כדרכי איש כי יושיע יי את עמו בידי ואתם
קומו ושובו לאהליכם:

36   וישמעו כל ישראל את התשועה אשר עשה יי על ידי קנז ויצאו לק<רא>תו
ויאמרו ברוך יי אשר הקימך לקצין בעמו כי עתה ידענו כי בחר יי
בעמו:

27.14= ויאמר קנז שאלו לאנשים אשר עמי את כל עמלי וישאלו להם ויאמרו חי
יי כי לא ידענו כי אם מצאנו את השדה מלא חללים:

37   ויאמר קנז אל שרי חמישיר לאמר הוציאו את האנשים האסורים ונשמע את
דבריהם ויוציאום ויבאו ויאמר להם קנז מה התלונות אשר הלינותם עלי
ויאמרו למה זה תשאל לנו ויי הסגירנו וצוה נא לשורפינו באש ולא על
התלונה כי אם על הראשונים אשר התודו את עונם ואנחנו לא נודענו
בעם וידינו עם החטאים ועל כן הסגירנו יי ויאמר קנז הן עתה
העידותם בנפשיכם ולמה אחדל מכם ויאמר לשורפם באש:

38   ויקרבו ימי קנז למות ויקרא לשני הנביאים אל פנחס ואל יבין וגם אל
פנחס בן אלעזר הכהן לאמר ידעתי את לב העם הזה כי ישובו מאחרי יי
ואעיד בהם:

28.3= ויאמר פנחס כאשר העד משה ויהושע כן העיד אבי בהם כי נתנבאו על
הכרם נטע שעשועי יי אשר לא ידע את נוטעו ולא יתברנו את אריסו
ונשחת הכרם ולא יטב פיריו ואלה הדברים אשר ציוני אבי לאמר לעם
הזה:

25The MS has לקנרתו; *LAB* has *obviam ei.*

27.12 And Kenaz returned to his army and found them sleeping, for a deep sleep fell upon them and they did not know what Kenaz had done by night. And they awoke from their sleep and saw all the field full of slain men and were very surprised. And Kenaz said: "Are the ways of the Lord like the ways of man? For the Lord will save his people by my hand. And you arise, and return to your tents."

27.13 And all Israel heard the salvation which the Lord worked by means of Kenaz and went out to meet him[25] and said: "Blessed is the Lord who appointed you as ruler among his people, for now we know that the Lord has chosen his people."

27.14 And Kenaz said: "Ask the men who are with me about all my labor." And they asked them, and they said: "As the Lord lives, we do not know anything except that we found the field full of slain men."

27.15 And Kenaz said to the captains of his fifties saying: "Bring out the men who are imprisoned, and we will hear their words." And they brought them out, and they came. And Kenaz said to them: "What are the murmurings which you murmured against me?" And they said: "Why do you ask us this, for the Lord has handed us over? Give the command, we pray, to burn us in the fire, and not on account of murmuring but as with the former men who confessed their iniquity. And we were not exposed among the people, but our hands were with the sinners. Therefore, the Lord handed us over." And Kenaz said: "Behold now you have testified against yourselves, and why should I spare you?" And he said to burn them in the fire.

[LAB 27.16 says that Kenaz ruled 57 years.]

28:1-2 And the days of Kenaz drew near for him to die, and he called the two prophets Phineas and Jabin and also Phineas son of Eleazar the priest saying: "I know the heart of this people, for they will turn from the Lord; and I testify against them."

28.3-4 And Phineas said: "As Moses and Joshua testified, so my father testified against them. For they prophesied about the vineyard, *the planting of the Lord's delight* (Isa 5.7) which did not know its planter and would not recognize its cultivator, and the vineyard was corrupted, and its fruit was not good. And these are the words which my father commanded me to say to this people."

28.5= וישא קנז את קולו בבכי וגם כל הזקנים והעם בכו בכי גדול עד הערב
ויאמרו הבעד עון הצאן נאבד הרועה ועתה יחמול יי על נחלתו ולא
יעמול לשוא:

39   ותהי רוח יי על קנז ויתנבא לאמר ראיתי את אשר לא קריתי ואביט
באשר לא חשבתי: שמעו נא יושבי הארץ המתנבאים לפניי הרואים את
הדור הזה טרם תשחת הארץ למען תדעו ותבינו בנבואות רבות אשר בארץ:

40   ועתה הנה אני רואה להבה אינה יוקדת ואשמע מקורות פרודות ויוצאות
בחלומי אשר אין להם יסוד ואין דרך בהרים להם ואין יסודתם באויר
כי אם נראו בתבניתם ומקום אין להם וכאשר העין לא ידע באשר יראה
הלב מה יבין:

41   מן הלהבה אשר אינה יוקדת ואראה והנה ניצוץ עלה ועמד באויר ועשה
מעמדו כמגן כעורג עכביש בקורה ואראה כי זה יסודו ויוציא מקורו
קצף רותח וישנה להיות ליסוד תהום ונתיבות בין יסוד עליון ליסוד
תחתון אשר שם תאיר אורה נעלמה וכדמות בני אדם הולכים בם ואשמע
קול אומר בין אלה היסודות ישבו בני האדם שבעת אלפי שנים:

28.9= ויבלה יסוד התחתון והעליון אשר הוא כקצף יהיה ליסוד והאורה אשר
ביניהם אשר תאיר לבני אדם על נתיבותם היא ירושלים ושם בני האדם
והיה כאשר יחטאו לי במלאות עת חטאתם תכבה הניצוץ ויבש המקור
ויעבירו כל:

42   ויהי בהנבא קנז כן ותשב רוח נפשו אליו והוא לא ידע מה דבר
בנבואתו ויאמר אל העם אם מנוחת הצדיקים אחרי מותם כן טוב להם
למות בילדותם בעולם הזה ולא יחטאו: וימת קנז ויקם עתניאל בנו
תחתיו:

[CJ 58.1-3 tells of Othniel, Ehud, Shamgar, Deborah and Barak.]

---

[26]The translation follows *LAB*'s *ipse* (= God).
[27]See *LAB omnes vos qui habitatis in ea*.

28.5   And Kenaz lifted up his voice in weeping, and also all the
        elders and the people wept a great weeping until evening.
        And they said: "Is it because of the iniquity of the flock
        that the shepherd is destroyed? And now may the Lord have
        pity on his inheritance, and let him[26] not labor in vain."

28.6   And the spirit of the Lord came upon Kenaz, and he prophesied
        saying: "I have seen what I did not expect and have viewed
        what I did not imagine. Hear, I pray, the inhabitants of the
        earth, those who prophesied before me, who were seeing this
        generation before the earth was corrupted in order that you
        may know and understand the many prophecies, you who are on
        the earth.[27]

28.7   And now behold I see a flame which is not burning, and I
        hear in my dream springs dividing into branches and going
        out which had no source and had no course in the mountains
        and had no base in the air, but they appeared in their form,
        and they had no place. And as the eye did not know what it
        should see, what would the heart understand?

28.8   From the flame which was not burning, I saw, and behold, a
        spark going up and stand in the air and take its position
        like a shield, like the twisting of a spider in its web. And
        I saw that this was its source, and its spring poured out
        boiling foam; and it was changed to be the base of the abyss, and
        there were paths between the upper base and the lower base
        where there shone the hidden light and beings like the sons of
        man were walking in them. And I heard a voice saying: 'Be-
        tween these bases ths sons of man will dwell for 7000 years.

28.9   And the lower base will be worn out, and the upper which is
        like foam will be the base. And its light which is between
        them which shines for the sons of man on their paths is Jeru-
        salem and there are the sons of man. And it will happen when
        they sin against me, when the time of their sinning is com-
        plete, the spark will be extinguished and the spring will dry
        up, and all will pass away."

28.10   And when Kenaz had prophesied in this way, the spirit of his
        soul returned to him, and he did not know what he said in his
        prophecy. And he said to the people: "If the rest of the
        just after their death is thus, it is better for them to die
        at their birth in this world and not sin." And Kenaz died,
        and Othniel his son arose in his place.

[LAB 29.1-31.2 tells of the exploits of Zebul (29) and the crises
facing Israel in the time of Deborah and Barak (30.1-31.1).]

58.4 וסיסרא בנס ברגליו אל אהל יעל כי יצאה לקראתו ותשקהו ותכסהו
ויישן וירדם: ותתפלל יעל אל יי ותאמר אנא יי החזק את אמתך באיבך
ובזה אדע אשר תמכרהו בידי אם אורידהו ממשכב ארצה ולא יקיץ ותעש
כן ותקח את יתד האהל ואת המקבת בידה ותתקע את היתד ברקתו כנבואת
דבורה: וילכד ברק את חצור ויהרג את מלכה ואת כל אשר בה:

5   ויהי בצאת סיסרא להלחם על ישראל ותקסם תמר אמו בקסמיה היא
ונערותיה ושרותיה לאמר כי סיסרא מנשי בני ישראל ומבנותיהם עם
צבעי רקמיהם ישלול לו כי ראתה בקסמיה כי ישכב במיטה יעל אשת חבר
ונתכסה ב‹ש› מיכה הוא מעיל מרוקם כצבעים ועל כן אמרה רחם רחמתים
לראש גבר:

[*CJ*58.6 gives chronological information and notes Gideon's succes-
sion as judge.]

7   מצאתי כי עוד שאל גדעון אות אחר כי אמר תן לי אות שבחר אותי
הקדוש להושיע את ישראל כאשר נתן יי למשה אשר הושיע את ישראל
ממצרים ויאמר לו המלאך רוץ והבא לי מים מן האגם ההוא ושפוך על
הצור הזה ואתן לך אות וירץ ויבא את המים ויאמר המלאך ש}ל{אל לך
אות אם אם דם אש יהיו המים ויען גדעון ויאמר מקצת המים יהיו אש
ומקצתם דם ויהי כן ולא כיבה הדם את האש וגם האש לא הוביש את הדם:
[*CJ* 58.8-9 provides further chronological information and Tola's suc-
cession.]

---

[1]Jdgs 4.17 and *CJ* have Sisera fleeing on foot; *LAB* has him
sedens equo.

[2]In *LAB* her name is Themech.

[3]The MT for Jdgs 4.18 spells with *śin*: בשׂמיכה, but the *CJ* MS
has *samek* בסמיכה.

[4]The MS has שלאל.

31.3-7 *And* when *Sisera* fled *on foot*[1] *to the tent of Jael* (Jdgs
    4.17), she went out to meet him and kissed him and covered
    him. And he slept and went into a deep slumber. And Jael
    prayed to the Lord and said: "Lord, I pray that you streng-
    then your handmaid against your enemy. And by this I will
    know that you will hand him over into my hand, if I bring him
    down from the bed to the ground and he does not wake up."
    And thus she did. *And she took the tent-peg and the hammer
    in her hand, and she drove the peg into his temple* (Jdgs
    4.21) according to the prophecy of Deborah. And Barak con-
    quered Hazor and killed its king and everyone who was there.

31.8   And when Sisera went out to fight against Israel, Tamar[2] his
    mother, she and her maidens and princesses, divined by her in-
    struments (see Jdgs 5.28) of divination saying that Sisera
    would take as plunder for himself from the wives of the sons
    of Israel and their daughters along with their embroidered
    dyed stuff, for she saw in her divinations that he would
    recline on the bed of Jael the wife of Heber and he would be
    covered with a coverlet[3] that is with an embroidered dyed
    robe and therefore she said: *"A maiden or two for every man
    ...."* (Jdgs 5.28-30).

[*LAB* 31.9-35.5 presents the hymn of Deborah (32), the death of
Deborah (33), the magical enticements of Aod (34) and the call of
Gideon (35.1-5).]

35.6-7 I find that Gideon asked for yet another sign, for he said:
    "Give me a sign (see Jdgs 6.17-21) that the Holy One has
    chosen me to save Israel as the Lord gave to Moses who saved
    Israel from the Egyptians." And the angel said to him: "Run
    and bring to me water from that pool, and pour it on this
    rock. And I will give you a sign." And he ran and brought
    the water, and the angel said: "Ask[4] the sign for yourself,
    whether the water will become blood or fire." And Gideon
    answered and said: "Part of the water will become fire, and
    part of it blood." And thus it was. And the blood did not
    extinguish the fire, and also the fire did not dry up the
    blood....

[*LAB* 36.1-37.5 tells of Gideon's victory (36) and the parable of
Jotham (37).]

10　ויקם אחריו יאיר הגלעדי ויעש יאיר מזבח לבעל ויפן ישראל אחריו
ויעבדו את הבעל לבד משבעה אנשים צדיקים אשר לא עבדוהו ואלה שמותם
ד̲פ̲ל ואבי יזרעאל גותיאל שלום אשחור יונדב שמעי:

38.2=　ויאמרו אל יאיר זכרנו את אשר צוה משה לישראל כשמרו לכם פן תסורו
מאחרי יי ואתה תשחת העם לעבד לבעל:

38.3=　ויצו יאיר לעבדיו לשרפם באש על אשר הגיו בבעל ויקחום וישליכום
באש ותצא האש מאתם ותשרף את עבדי יאיר אשר השליכום וכל בית יאיר:
והאנשים שבעה יצאו מן האש והלכו לדרכם כי האנשים אשר סביבותיהם
הוכו בסנוירים ולא ראו אותם:

38.4=　ותגע האש עד בית יאיר וישמע יאיר את קול יי אומר הקימותך לשופט על
ישראל ותשחת את העם לסור מאחר ולעבד לבעל והם הדבקים בי שרפת באש
המה יחיר ואתה תמות בשריפת אש אשר לא תכבה עוד וישרף יי את יאיר
ואת ביתו ואת הבעל ועשרת אלפי איש עמו ויקבר יאיר בקמון:

[CJ 58.11 records the capture of Helen as well as that of Castor and
Pollux, the building of Carthage, and the invention of the Latin
alphabet.]

---

[5]In *LAB* there is a gap of uncertain length between the end of
37.5 and the start of 38.1.

[6]*LAB* has two names in one:　Abiesdrel.

[7]*LAB* has Memihel.

[8]Perhaps we can suppose:　כ.(אשר אמר) שמרו

[9]*LAB* has *blasphemaverunt*.　Perhaps, read הגידו.

38.1   *And Jair*[5] *the Gileadite rose up after him* (Jdgs 10.3).   And
       Jair made an altar to Baal, and Israel turned in its direction.
       And they served Baal, except for seven righteous men who did
       not worship him.   And these are their names: Dapal and Abi
       Yezre"el,[6] Gûtî'el, Šalôm, 'Ašḥûr, Yônadab, Šim'î.[7]

38.2   And they said to Jair: "We remember what Moses commanded
       Israel when (he said):[8] 'Watch yourselves, lest you turn
       from the Lord and you corrupt the people to serve Baal.'"

38.3   And Jair commanded his servants to burn them in the fire be-
       cause they spoke[9] against Baal, and they took them and cast
       them into the fire. But the fire went away from them and
       burned the servants of Jair, who had cast them in, and all
       the household of Jair. And the seven men went out from the
       fire and went on their way, for the men who were around them
       were struck with sudden blindness and did not see them.

38.4   And the fire reached the house of Jair, and Jair heard[10] the
       voice of the Lord saying: "I have appointed you judge over
       Israel, and you have corrupted the people to turn away and
       to serve Baal. And those who cling to me, you have burned in
       the fire. Those will live, but you will die in the burning
       fire which will not be extinguished again." And the Lord
       burned Jair and his house and the Baal and 10000 men with
       him. And Jair *was buried in Qamôn* (Jdgs 10.5).

[*LAB* 39.1-6 includes Jephthah's prayer of petition.]

---

[10]Perhaps we should emend to וישמע.

59.1   ויקם אחרי יאיר יפתח הגלעדי אשר הושיע ישראל מיד בני עמון:

=39.7   ויתפלל יפתח וכל ישראל לפני יי במצפה לאמר אנא יי הושיעה נא ואל
        תתן נחלתך להרג ואת כרמך למפציה ופקוד נא את הגפן אשר נטעת והסעת
        אותה ממצרים:

=39.8   וישלח יפתח מלאכים אל גַתָאַל מלך בני עמון לאמר מה לי ולך כי באתה
        אלי וגו':

2   ותהי על יפתח רוח יי ויצא להלחם את בני עמון וידר יפתח נדר ליי
        ויאמר אם נתון תתן את בני עמון בידי והיה יורא מדלתי ביתי לקראתי
        בשובי בשלום מבני עמון והיה ליי והעליתיהו עולה:

=40.1   ויך יפתח את בני עמון ויכנעו מפני ישראל וישב יפתח מצפתה והנה כל
        הבתולות והנשים יצאו לקראתו בתופים ובמחולות ותצא בתו ראשוני
        לקראתו ורק היא יחידה ואין לו ממנו בן או בת:

3   ויהי כראותה ויקרע את בגדיו ויאמר אהה בתי הכרע הכרעתני ואת היית
        בעכרי ומי יתן ל[25 ±]יס ואראה מי יכריע כי הד⟨אב⟩תיני במשתה
        שמחת ניצחון מלחמותיי ואנכי פציתי פי אל יי ולא אוכל לשוב:

4   ותאמר לו שְׁאֵילַה בתו על מה דאבת על מיתתי אחרי אשר עשה יי לך
        נקמות מאיביך: אך זכור נא את אבותינו אשר האב העלה את הבן לעולה
        ונתרצו המקריב והנקרב:

---

[1]MT has היורצא אשר יצא while LXX, *LAB* and Vulgate omit אשר יצא.

[2]There is space for about 25 letters. *LAB* here has *Et nunc
quis dabit [cor meum in statera et animam in pondere, et stabo] et
videbo....*

[3]The MS has incorrectly הדבאתיני.

39.6   And after Jair Jephthah the Gileadite, who saved Israel from
        the hand of the sons of Ammon, arose.

39.7   And Jephthah and all Israel prayed before the Lord in Mizpah
        saying: "Lord, we pray, save us, we beg; and do not give
        your inheritance over to the slaughter and your vineyard to
        those who would scatter it. And tend, we pray, the vine
        which you planted and led out from Egypt.

39.8   *And Jephthah sent messengers to* Gete'al *king of the sons of
        Ammon saying: "What is there between me and you that you
        have come to me* (Jdgs 11.12), etc.?"

[*LAB* 39.8-9 presents an exchange of messages between Jephthah and
Gete'al.]

39.10   And the Spirit of the Lord came upon Jephthah, and he went
        out to fight the sons of Ammon. *And Jephthah vowed a vow to
        the Lord and said: "If indeed you give the sons of Ammon
        into my hand, then whoever goes out*[1] *from the doors of my
        house to meet me when I return in peace from the sons of
        Ammon will be the Lord's, and I will offer it as a holocaust"*
        (Jdgs 11.30-31).

[*LAB* 39.11 tells of God's anger at Jephthah's foolish vow.]

40.1   And Jephthah smote the sons of Ammon, and they were humbled
        before Israel. And Jephthah returned to Mizpah, *and behold
        all the virgins and women went out to meet him with timbrels
        and with dances. And his daughter went out first to meet him.
        And she was his only child; and beside her he had neither son
        nor daughter.*
        And when he saw her, *he rent his garments and said: "Alas my
        daughter, you have brought me very low, and you have been a
        source of great trouble to me* (Jdgs 11.34-35). And who will
        put [± 25   ][2] and I will see which will go down.
        For you have made me faint[3] at the feast celebrating my vic-
        tories in battle. *And I have opened my mouth to the Lord,
        and I cannot take it back."*

40.2   And Šᵉ'êlah his daughter said to him: "Why do you faint over
        my death *after the Lord has exacted for you revenge from your
        enemies* (Jdgs 11.36)? But remember, I pray, our fathers that
        the father offered the son as a holocaust (see Gen 22), and
        both the sacrificer and the sacrificed were received with
        favor.

40.3= כן עשה לי אבי כאשר יצא מפיך: אך שאלה אחת אשאלך בטרם אמות הרפה

ממני שנים חדשים ואתפללה לאשר אשיב את נפשי ואלכה וירדתי אל

ההרים ואלינה בגבעות ואדרכה בסלעים ואבכה על בתולי אני ורעותיי

ואשפכה עליהם דמעותיי ואקרר דאגת ילדותיי ויבכוני עצי השדה

ויספדוני חיות שדי כי לא דאבתי במיתתי ולא ידאבני משיבי נפשי

בפיצת פי אבי אשר נדרני לזבוח ליי: אך כי יראתי אשר לא יתקבל

קרבן נפשי לרצון ותהי מיתתי חנם:

5   ויעש לה כן אביה ותלך היא ורעותיה ותספר לחכמי עמה ואין משיב לה

דבר ותעל להרי תֶלֶג ויזכריה יי בלילה ויאמר הנה נא סכרתי את פי

חכמי עמי אשר לא ענו דבר לבת יפתח ועתה יותן נפש⟨ה⟩ כשאלתה

וחמות שלה יקר בעיני כי חכמת החכמת לה:

6   ותבא שְׁאִילָה בת יפתח ותשטח בחיק אמה:

40.5= ותלך ותבכה בהרי תלג ותספוד ותאמר שמעו הרים מספד תאנותיי

והקשיבו גבעות את דמעי עיניי וצורי הסלעים תעידו בבכי נפשי איכה

נמסרה נפשי למות ולא לחנם נפשי: יתכפרו דבריי בשמים ויתכתבו

דמעותיי ברקיע כי לא ⟨ר⟩חם האב את הבת אשר נדר אותה להקריב וגם

אל שריו לא שמע כי אמר יחידתו להקריב:

40.6= ואנכי לא ראיתי מחופתי ולא נמלאה כתר נשואיי ולא לבשתי פארי עדיי

כלה היושבת בבתוליה ולא הוקטרתי במור ואהל ריח ניחוח:

---

[4]MT has על.

[5]תֶלֶג in Aramaic means "snow"; Targum Onkelos on Deut 3.9 calls
Mt. Hermon the "mountain of snow." *LAB* has *Stelac*.

[6]The MS has נפשי.

[7]MT has המוחה.

[8]All *LAB* MSS except K and P (usually the best!) have *et abiens
decidet in sinum matrum suarum*.

[9]We have emended MS נלחם to רחם, but *LAB* does have *expugnet (ut
pater non expugnet filiam quam devovit sacrificare....)*.

[10]In translation I follow P. M. Bogaert's emendation of *LAB
sedens in genua mea* to *sedens in genicio meo* where *genicio* comes
from *gynaecium* (= "woman's quarters").

40.3   Therefore, *do to me*, my father, *according to the word that went forth from your mouth*. But one request I ask you before I die. *Let me alone two months*, and let me pray to the one to whom I will return my soul. *And let me go and wander about*[4] *the mountains* and lodge in the hills and make my way in the cliffs *and bewail my virginity, I and my companions* (Jdgs 11.36-37). And I will pour out my tears upon them and will cool the grief of my youth. And the trees of the field will bewail me, and the beasts of the field will lament me. For I did not faint over my death and it did not make me faint to return my soul when my father opened his mouth and vowed to sacrifice me to the Lord. But I am afraid that the offering of my soul will not be accepted as pleasing and my death will be for nought."

40.4   And her father did this for her. And she and her companions went. And she told the wise men of her people, but no one answered a word to her. And she went up to mountains of T^elag,[5] and the Lord remembered her by night and said: "Behold, I pray, I have shut the mouth of the wise men of my own people who did not answer a word to the daughter of Jephthah. Now ⟨her⟩[6] soul will be given over according to her request, *and her death*[7] *is precious in my eyes* (Ps 116.15) for she has supreme wisdom."
And Še'êlah the daughter of Jephthah came and lay flat on the bosom of her mother.[8]

40.5   And she went and wept in the mountains of T^elag, and she lamented and said: "Hear, mountains, the lament over my coupling; and give heed, hills, to the tears of my eyes; and, you rocks of the cliffs, bear witness to the weeping of my soul. Alas, my soul has been handed over to death, but not for naught. My words will be atoned for in the heavens, and my tears inscribed on the firmament, for the father who vowed to sacrifice his daughter did not ⟨ have mercy on ⟩[9] her and also did not heed his captains but intended to sacrifice his only daughter.

40.6   But I have not looked out from my bridal canopy, and my wedding crown is not completed. And I have not put on the beautiful adornments of a bride sitting in her woman's quarters,[10] and I have not been perfumed with myrrh and sweet-smelling aloes,

7   ולא נמשחתי בשמן המשחה אשר נכון לי: אהה אמי לשוא ילידתיני הנה
     יחידתך בשאול חופתה אך שוא יגעת בי בשמן משחתיני ולבנים
     הלביש‹ו›ני כי }עס ו{סס יאכלם ופרחי כתרי באשר גדלתני יבלו
     ריבשר ובגדיי המרוקמים בתכלת וארגמן רימה ישחיתם ועתה יאנחו
     ריעותיי כל ימי מספדי:

40.7= ריטו העצים פארוחם ובדיהם ויבכו כל בתוליי ויבאו חית יער וירמסו
     על בתוליי כי נגזרו שנותיי וימי חיי בחשך יעתיקו:

8   ריהי מקץ שנים חדשים ותשב אל אביה ריעש לה את נדרו אשר נדר ותבאו
     בתולי ישראל ויקברוה ויספדוה ותהי חוק בישראל   מימים ימימה
     תלכנה בנות ישראל לתנות לבת יפתח ארבעה ימים בשנה:

[CJ 59.8-11 discusses the death of Hercules, more judges in Israel,
the capture of Troy and the founding of Rome.]

12   ריעש מיכה כל אשר צותה אמו אותו ריעש לו שלש צלמי אדם ושלשה צלמי
     עגלים ודמות נשר וארי ותנין: והיה כל מבקש לשאל לבנים יבקש
     מצלמי אדם והמבקש לעושר יבקש מן הנשר ומבקש לגבורה מן האריה
     ומבקש לבנים (ו)לבנות מן העגלים ומבקש לאורך ימים מן התנין
     והמבקש מכל דבר יבקש מן היונה:

44.6= ריזנו כל בית ישראל אחריהם ויעזבו את יי ויעבדום וימכרם יי ביד
     עמי הארץ וישובו ויפקדם יי לעתים:

_____

[11]The MS has הלבישיני.
[12]יעס ור may be merely a false start; *LAB* has *tinea* only.
[13]חדשים is supralinear but certain from the biblical text.
[14]We have added *waw*; *LAB* has *pro pueris et pro puellis*.

and have not been anointed with the oil of anointing which is
prepared for me. Alas, my mother, in vain have you given
birth to me. Behold your only daughter - her bridal canopy
is in Sheol. But in vain have you toiled for me with the oil
you anointed me! The white garments which clothed me,[11] the
moth[12] will devour them. And the sprouts of my crown with
which you exalted me will wear out and dry up, and my garments
embroidered in blue and purple the worm will destroy. And
now my companions will bemoan all the days of my lamenting.

40.7   And trees will stretch out their boughs and their limbs, and
all will weep over my virginity. And the beasts of the forest
will come and trample on my virginity, for my years are cut
off and the days of my life will move forward in darkness.

40.8   *And at the end of two months*[13] *she returned to her father and
he fulfilled with her his vow which he vowed.* And the vir-
gins of Israel came and buried her and lamented her. *And it
became a custom in Israel that year by year the daughters of
Israel came to lament the daughter of Jephthah the Gileadite
four days in the year* (Jdgs 11.39-40).

[*LAB* 40.9-44.4 tells of Jephthah's death (40.9), the judgeships of
Addo and Elon (41), the promise of Samson (42), the birth of Samson
(43), and the rise of Micah (44.1-4)]

44.5   And Micah did everything which his mother commanded him. And
he made for himself three images of man and three images of
calves and the likeness of an eagle and a lion and a serpent.
And everyone seeking to ask for sons would seek them from the
images of man; and one seeking for wealth would seek it from
the eagle; and one seeking for strength, from the lion; and
one seeking for sons (and)[14] daughters, from the calves; and
one seeking for a long life, from the serpent; and one seeking something of everything would seek it from the dove.

44.6   And all the house of Israel went astray after them and for-
sook the Lord and served them. And the Lord handed them over
to the peoples of the land; and they repented, and the Lord
visited them at intervals.

[*LAB* 44.6-46.1 continues the Lord's speech with its emphasis on the
Decalogue (44.6-10), the murder of the concubine (45) and the search
for a course of action (46.1).]

13   ויהי כאשר עלו בני ישראל על שבט הדני למלחמה על אודות הפלגש אשר

מתה בגבעה ויתנגפו בני ישראל לפני בני דן וישחיתו בישראל ביום

ההוא שנים ועשרים (אלף) איש:

46.3=   ויעלו בני ישראל ויבכו לפני יי עד הערב ויאמרו נשאלה ביי לאמר

במה העון הזה אשר כשלנו וישאלו ביי לאמר האוסיף לגשת למלחמה עם

בני בנ⟨ימ⟩ן אחי ויאמר יי עלו אליו ואחר אודיעכם במה יכשלו העם

ויצאו ביום השיני להלחם עם בנימן וישחיתו בבני ישראל עוד שמונת

עשר אלף איש:

46.4=   ויעלו כל ישראל ביתאל כי שם ארון ברית יי ויבכו ויצומו ביום ההוא

עד הערב ויעלו עולות ושלמים לפני יי:

14   ויתפלל פנחס בן אלעזר הכהן לפני יי ויאמר יי אלהים אם יישר

בעיניך את אשר עשו בני בנימן למה השאת אותנו בהם לנפול בידם ואם

רע בעיניך את אשר עשו למה נפלנו לפניהם:

47.1=   הגד נא לעבדך במי העון הזה ונטיבה לך כי הנני זוכר את אשר עשיתי:

דקרתי את זמרי בקנאתי והצלתני מיד עמו והרגת בהם ארבעה

ועשרים אלף:

47.2=   ואתה עתה אמרת לשבטי ישראל עלו להלחם את בנימן:

15   וישמע יי בקול פנחס ויאמר ⟨הקנאתי⟩ קנאו לי בני ישראל בנבלה הזאת

ולא קנאו לי בפסל מיכה אשר עשה להזנות את כל ישראל אחריו: על כן

קנאתי ונקמתי בישראל כי נבהלו על פלגש אחת לבער עשה נבלה ולא

בערו את עובדי פסל מיכה: ועתה אסיפו בני ישראל לעלות למלחמה עם

בנימין ומחר אתננו ביד⟨כם⟩:

---

[15]According to *LAB* and Jdgs 20.12-13 this should be Benjamin
(as it is as *CJ*'s story unfolds).

[16]אלף must be supplied; *LAB* has *quadragintaquinque milia virorum*
but MT and *CJ* agree.

[17]The MS has בנמין.

[18]Again *CJ* agrees with MT; *LAB* has *quadraginta sex milia viro-rum*.

[19]The MS has הקנאתי קנאו, but הקנאתי seems to be a false start
or perhaps we should read בקנאתי "with jealousy for me."

[20]The MS has בידי; *LAB* has *Tradam vobis illos*.

46.2   And when the sons of Israel went up for battle against the
        tribe of Dan[15] on account of the concubine who died in Gibeah
        (see Jdgs 20.12-13), the sons of Israel were smitten before
        the sons of Dan and they destroyed in Israel on that day
        22000 (twenty-two (thousand))[16] men (see Jdgs 20.21).

46.3   *And the sons of Israel went up and wept before the Lord until
        evening*, and they said: "Let us ask the Lord, saying: 'What
        is this iniquity through which we have stumbled?'" And they
        asked the Lord, *saying: "Shall I continue to draw near for
        battle with the sons of Benjamin*[17] *my brother?" And the Lord
        said: "Go up against him* (Jdgs 20.23), and later I will in-
        form you why the people stumbles." And they went out on the
        second day to fight with Benjamin, *and they destroyed among
        the sons of Israel* 18000[18] *more men* (Jdgs 20.25).

46.4   *And all Israel went up to Bethel* because *there was the ark* of
        the covenant of the Lord, *and they wept and fasted on that
        day until evening. And they offered holocausts and peace-
        offerings before the Lord* (Jdgs 20.26-28).
        And Phineas the son of Eleazar the priest prayed before the
        Lord and said: "Lord God, if what the sons of Benjamin have
        done is right in your eyes, why did you bring us against them
        to fall into their hands; and if what they did is wrong in
        your eyes, why have we fallen before them?

47.1   Tell, I pray, your servant in whom is this iniquity, and we
        will do what pleases you. For, behold, I remember what I
        did - I speared Zimri in my zeal (see Num 25.6-18) - and
        you saved me from the weapons of his people and killed among
        them 24000.

47.2   But you now have said to the tribes of Israel: 'Go up to
        fight Benjamin.'"

47.3-   And the Lord heard the voice of Phineas and said: "The sons
  12   of Israel were zealous[19] for my sake in regard to this corpse,
        but they were not zealous for my sake in regard to Micah's
        idol which he made to lead astray all Israel after him.
        Therefore I was zealous and took revenge in Israel, for they
        were disturbed about one concubine so as to burn out the one
        responsible for the corpse, but they did not burn out the
        makers of Micah's idol. And now gather, you sons of Israel,
        to go up for battle with Benjamin, and tomorrow I will give
        him into <your> hand."[20]

16   ויעלו ויגוף יי את בנימן לפני ישראל ויפלו מבנימן שמונה עשר אלף
איש ויהי כל הנפלים מבנימן עשרים וחמשה איש אלף ויונסו שש מאות
איש אל סלע הרמון ונמלטו וינחמו בני ישראל בנימן אחיו והיה שלום
לנותרים וישובו לנחלתם ויבנו את הערים וישבו בם ובני ישראל הלכו
איש לשבטו ואיש לנחלתו:

17   ויקרבו ימי פנחס למות ויאמר יי אליו בן מאה ועשרים שנה אתה היום
אשר הם ימי האדם ועתה קום ולך לך אל הרי ושב שם ימים רבים ואצוה
שם את ה{י}ערבים לכלכלך ואל נשריי ואל תרד לבני אדם עד געת קץ
ואז תסגור השמים ובפיך יפתח ואחר תתנשא במקום אשר נתנשאו אבותיך
רשם תהיה עד אשר אזכור את העולם:

=48.2   ויעש פנחס בן אלעזר הכהן כאשר צוהו יי:

[CJ 60.1-100.5 continues the history of Israel down to the death of
Judah the Maccabee.]

21In the MS שנה is written twice.
22The MS היערבים must be modified to הערבים.
23LAB mentions the eagle only (aquile mee).

And they went up, and the Lord smote Benjamin before Israel.
And from Benjamin there fell 18000 men, *and all those fallen
from Benjamin were 25000 men*. And 600 men fled *to the cliff
of Rimmon* (Jdgs 20.46-47), and they escaped. And the sons of
Israel had pity on Benjamin their brother, and there was
peace for the survivors. And they returned to their inherit-
ance and built cities and dwelt in them. And the sons of
Israel went, each man to his tribe and each man to his in-
heritance.

48.1   And the days of Phineas drew near to die, and the Lord said
to him: "You are 120 years[21] old today which equals the days
of man's life. And now rise up and go by yourself to my
mountain, and remain there many days. And there I will command the ravens (see 1 Kgs 17.4)[22] to supply you (and also my
eagles).[23] But do not descend to the sons of man until the
appointed time has arrived. And then you will close the
heavens, and at your word they will open. And afterwards you
will be lifted up to the place where your fathers are lifted
up, and there you will be until I remember the world."

48.2   And Phineas son of Eleazar the priest did as the Lord commanded him.

[*LAB* 48.3-65.5 continues the history of Israel down to the death of
Saul.]

INDEX OF SCRIPTURAL REFERENCES

The numbers following the scriptural texts refer to the text of *CJ*; those in parentheses refer to *LAB*.

74

Index